D1430865

ONE-UPMANSHIP

One-upmanship

by

STEPHEN POTTER

ILLUSTRATIONS BY LT. COL. FRANK WILSON

Being Some Account of the
Activities and Teaching of the
LIFEMANSHIP CORRESPONDENCE COLLEGE OF
ONE-UPNESS AND GAMESLIFEMASTERY

New York   HENRY HOLT AND COMPANY

FIRST EDITION

Library of Congress Catalog Card Number:
52-11048

To Andrew and Julian

Contents

vii

CONTENTS

CONTENTS

PART ONE

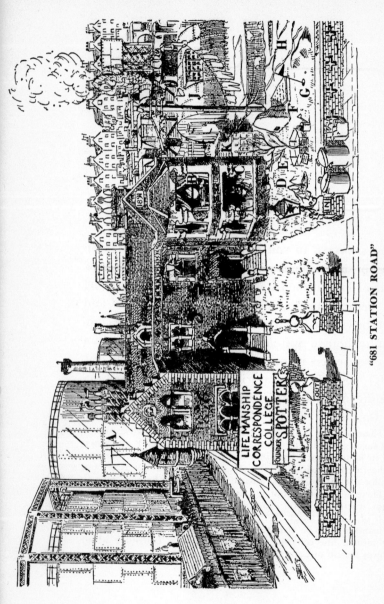

"681 STATION ROAD"

Note in this recent drawing (A) dummy television aerial, (B) Founder's bedroom, (C) dining hall with separate tables, (D) eucalyptus tree planted by former member of staff, Miss C. Johnson, (E) eucalyptus tree planted by Founder, (F) sheer rock for Rockmanship, (G) ordinary putting green, (H) lawn tennis court (vicarage type), (J) museum of Clothesmanship (presented by the Harvard Foundation and Mellon Trust), (K) dummy conserva-tory.

I

Our College

I AM SPEAKING to you now [1] as newly elected President of the Lifemanship Correspondence College. When I look at the list of distinguished names among our helpers and founders here I am astonished and even bewildered at the honour. Ours is a small community, housed quite modestly in a converted section of a converted mansion, yet from the files and the class-rooms, the laboratories and the libraries, Lifemanship throws its lifeline from Alaska in the West to Colchester in the East.[2] Linked by vast sea

[1] These opening words form part of a lecture first delivered to a very small group in the waiting room of Mark's Tey Railway Station in January, 1952. I am indebted to Sir Ford Boulder, chairman of the catering division of the Great Eastern Railway, as it once was, for not withholding permission to print them here.

[2] There is as yet no Games-Life Association at Frinton, for instance, where one would expect it. Although a happy and natural result of the Aldeburgh Festival has been the founding of a small Lifemanship Club in that resort, it may be said that the Games-Life median line coincides unexpectedly with a Longitude which involves the tip of Cape Cod, famed in Melville.

routes,[3] it has been said of Lifemanship that we have been called into being in the role of the Old World redressing the balance of the New World redressing the balance of the Old.

But let me tell you something of our small self-contained University, not a thousand miles from Yeovil. Students from Wyoming, it is true, cannot reach us here. With them we deal, inevitably, by letter. For such, Correspondence College it must be; yet we prefer and welcome the personal touch, the human problem in the flesh; we are proud of the young lads and lasses who come to L.C.C. to study at first hand.

We boast no domes nor pediments. In spite of Gamesmanship Rallies and GIVE FREELY TO LIFEMANSHIP weeks, our dream of a worthy Senate House, built in Reinforced Functional Revival, waits fulfilment.[4] Every penny of our endowment is spent on equipment and it is spent on staff.

I should like to describe to you our work rooms—yes, and our play rooms as well, not unlike those of one of the older Universities, with whom we coexist in mutual evaluation and respect.

Here a room which belongs to the Arts Faculty, at first like any other such; but look again, and see how, in a detail, Lifemanship's doctrine of One-upness is

[3] *Note:* It is estimated that eleven-twelfths of Lifemanship's vast "Empire" is covered by water.

[4] We still await the government grant due to our foundation.

4

always followed or imbued. Note the piano with cigarette stains on the upper notes. But these are dummy surfaces removable at will, because it is not in all company that such signs of Bohemian inconsequence impress.

There is the conductor's baton—but where is the Orchestra? In the gramophone cabinet, for it is the conducting of gramophone records which we teach, splendid way to corner attention and cause confused irritation when music is being played.

Look too at the wall devoted to pictures. But how are they arranged? "O.K." in gold letters denotes "O.K. to praise this year." On the right, in black, "Ex O.K."—pictures which were O.K. ten years ago and which students must learn therefore to discard, for one-upness in pictureship.

See, too, our Modern Languages Department. On the left of the blackboard, correct French; on the right, French translated into English French, phonetically transcribed, a dialect which our students are taught to cultivate with aristocratic downrightness and amusingly insular don't-care-a-damnmanship.

Here on this white tablecloth made of indiarubber, coffee-spilling is taught in our Mannership cadre, with demonstrations of how to apologise, or not to, and how alternatively to engineer, as host, the awk-

5

ward pause and the "Don't-give-it-another-thought" sequence. (Lydall's Reproach.)

In the Gamesmanship section, take a glimpse, now. That strangely shaped racket is a tennis racket, for use in study or office where court tennis strokes may be demonstrated to players who are merely lawn.

And why the two lawn-tennis courts? Note that A (left) is humpy, wobbly, the net sagging and stringy, tied to unsuitable stick. On the right (B), all is taut and accurate, a Wimbledonship atmosphere, with all-steel umpire's chair and chromium seats for linesmen. It is here that lawn-tennis gambits *interchangeably suited to the contrasted gamesacre and lifeclimate of the two different courts* are worked out in detail. On this adjoining putting green, the now famous intimidation plays and distraction gambits for putters were first taught to men who have since won success in this field on courses as far removed as Studland or Little Canaan. Nearby, in that asphalt corner, see stacked the rubber rapiers of our fencers with the special "BRUZELESS" boxing gloves for students who need to say of this sport too in later life, "I once did a bit of it." That sheer three foot of plaster rock is for the rockman (see p. 132)—the mattress underneath is pneumatic and shockproof.

The seeming shed beyond is in fact the Museum of Clothesmanship, with "Right" and the equally Life-manlike and gambitous "Wrong" clothes standing

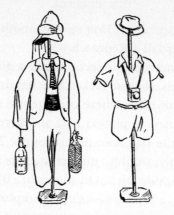

MUSEUM OF CLOTHESMANSHIP
For landing in Nairobi.
Wrong (left)   Right (right).

adjacent for amusement and instruction. Right and Wrong for grouse-shooting, for visiting a coal mine, for the Tate Gallery, for New Year's Eve, for landing in Nairobi.[5] And then, of course, I would show you the College Dining Hall, the Antisocial room, and the library, with its dummy books.

I want the pages which follow to be regarded as an introduction to Correspondence College techniques. It may be asked—why am I revealing all this? But we are not a money-making concern—primarily. If students are attracted by this glimpse of our methods, we shall welcome them. If not, let them admit that

[5] Oh, and countless others.

7

Lifemanship is not for them. I have seen some parents ruin many a natural Lifeboy by trying to force our philosophy on him when, at six or seven, he was too young, or too obstinate, to receive it.

Nor will I have it said that there is any mystery about ordinary Lifemanship, even if for obvious reasons its more advanced methods are known to initiates only. There are of course certain Supergambits known only to Yeovil, and though we are in full and free consultation with Washington and the Pentagon on the possibilities of their exploitation, the technique of these is still our secret. Therefore it is I suppose not surprising that at the time of going to press, the newspapers are full of an incident for which some will revile us, though others have shown sympathy. A well-known and even liked member of our staff has disappeared. His name—G. Wert. Never high in our confidence, he was yet a leading instructor in our Department of Foreign Enthusiasm, and an expert in Round Tableship and the Exchange of Unpleasantries. Last certainly seen at Ghent (office of our *L'Institution Vie-heureuse*), glimpsed at Algiers, he probably passed, as a shadow, over the Peloponnesian border and disappeared behind the Iron Curtain. Wherever he is, he has taken his secrets with him, and we now suffer the chagrin of listening, at Round Table conferences, to elementary Lifegambits from—why not name them?—the Russians. Thus has been inaugurated the era of Marxmanship in the conferences between East and West. Small wonder that the study of Lifemanship and Counter-lifemanship is regarded now as the still more urgent need of all of us.

Universityship.

L.C.C. (Lifemanship Correspondence College) is no substitute for three years' academic study at one of the older universities, and we have never made this claim. What we do intend, in our six weeks' course, is that the student should learn how to be top student, and, when he is launched on the world, how to become the postgraduate top post.

To help us in our work here, university groups form spontaneously, send us their suggestions, or just write saying "How to help?"

When I get these letters from young Lifestudents, many of them little more than Lifeboys, from Professors, too, of all denominations, my answer to the question is always "Write about *yourself,* how *you* got away with it, how *you* think it is possible to get by the examiners without actually cheating. Express *yourself.*"

Why the Silence of Yale?

The response, entirely unsolicited, has been extraordinary. Oxford and Cambridge have helped with

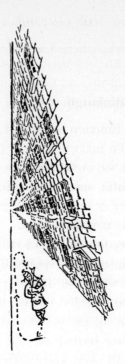

EDINBURGH, 1851

While his friends are working late on the night before the examination, fellow student distracts them by playing bagpipes outside their windows. Amazing that this example of primitive gamemanship took place *in the year of the Great Exhibition.*

their maturer views; Edinburgh, Bangor, and Leeds, in that order, have been perhaps more brilliantly experimental. Stanford, California, is at work, and Harvard has been especially forward with advice and publication. From Yale—I just want to record this as

10

a simple statement—there has been no communication whatever.

The Harvard-Edinburgh.

It has been our function to sift and co-ordinate these contributions. To make it clearer to new readers it can be said that we include in our studies the study of study, and fulfil our function as University University. It is the science of Scientific Attitudeship which we teach; the art of Arts.

I head this section "Harvard-Edinburgh" because it will serve to introduce a specifically *Universityship* study theme on which we like to prove our mettle— the basic approach, really, to the examination room. How to be one up on the lay student before the examinations have started; or how (passmanship) to excel after it is all over. Edinburgh specialises in the former; Harvard in the latter.

The phrase "to Edinburgh" implies a dissemination of despondency among other students working for Lifeman's examination by an appearance of solid knowledge, of calmness in the face of approaching crisis, and of a desire to help. In his inaugural address, as Senior President, to the Edinburgh University Lifemanship Research Group,[6] J. Weatherhead was particularly careful to stress the fact (to use his

[6] 29 January 1951.

11

own words) that the Undergraduateman must give one or two impressions, either that (1) he does nothing but work or (2) that he does no work. Concentrating on (1) he describes the work of J. Reid, who specialises in striding into the reading-room with his hat on, going "straight to the shelves of a subject he is not necessarily studying," [7] taking a book out as if he knew where to look for it, running down a reference, and walking out again *quietly but plonkingly*.

Over the faces of student watchers nervousness runs like a whisper; though in fact Reid has just picked up a book of quotations to verify a clue in a crossword puzzle. By an accumulation of such featherweight ploys as these,[8] Reid was able to oppress his fellow students with a sense of the hopelessness of any effort of theirs in the face of such competition, and many a promising degree man is virtually failed before he has set foot in the examination room.

"To Harvard" is, conversely, to seem, even when the examination is only two days off, to be totally indifferent to the impending crisis, and be seen walking calmly and naturally about, out of doors, enjoying the scenery and taking deep breaths of air.[9]

[7] Wider Interests Ploy.

[8] I believe that after putting the book back Reid sometimes speaks quietly to a shy-looking girl student *seeming to impart information to her,* as if to help her.

[9] *"Don't Harvard,"* I once, when a visitor to Worcester, Oxford, heard, during a pleasant outing with the Chameleon Club, shouted

Naturally many Edinburgh men also Harvard, and vice versa. But to maintain the truly contemporary nature of their native gambit, Harvard has its own special team—most of them on the teaching staff—with whom I am kept in touch.[10] A recent formulation is that of J. Smail's. This is Smail's wording. ("FitzJames" is a fictitious name.)

Famed Harvardman (as distinct from Harvard man) J. FitzJames disappeared suddenly from College midway through January Reading Period, just about the time his friends began studying in earnest. Then, on the day of his first exam, he would return, strolling into the examination room five minutes late, dressed in a light Palm Beach suit and heavily tanned. Sitting down next to a friend he would inspect his papers casually, and begin to write slowly.

Later it becomes known that FitzJames has received an A in the course. What is the explanation? FitzJames has been holing himself up in a miserable rented room in Boston surrounded by the total reading assignment including the optional books, and has been working like a dog for three weeks, stripped to the waist between two sun lamps.

A certain sum of money has been allocated at Harvard for the preparation of a counter to this gambit. Even if the results arrive too late to be printed in this

---

after an undergraduate who, walking to the bathroom on or about June 18, was humming.

[10] See *Harvard Alumni Bulletin*, 3 February 1952.

volume, I believe that by concentrating on an aspect of *one* of our activities, Universityship, I have given readers some insight into the *whole*.

II

Doctorship (M.D.manship), Patientship, and the Health Ploy

I BELIEVE that our College treatment of Medicine illustrates our aims and methods as well as any. Basic medical studentship, doctorship, and patientship provide us with the three "Threes" of Lifemanship teaching. Medical studentship is perhaps too advanced for the lay reader, and we have transposed to the end of the chapter a technical note on the work of Canada in this sphere.

Our ten days' course for young doctors—how different, in its brevity, compression, and point, from the seven *years* of grinding work in the more orthodox schools of medical education. Not that this latter must be neglected, but we do claim that in our Demonstrator in Harleyship and our Sir J. Boots Reader we have two extraordinarily fine men who can give a helping hand both during and after the period of academic study, not only in the simple Health ploys but also in the establishment of one-up relations between doctor and doctor and doctor and patient and vice versa.

Health and the Normal Lifeplay.

Ordinary *health*, remember, is highly gambit-prone. Novice Lifemen are often seen sparring with each other in the friendly cut and thrust of the Health move.

"It's only a scratch" is often the first Life-remark of the prattling Lifechild, and the reply made by the infant only slightly less young ("Well, that is a good fing anyhow") is often the first counter.

In later life it is soon discovered that a slight disability, properly used, can be advantageous, particularly where a desire to live up to a reputation for genius is required. We demonstrate the imperious stammer, the attention-inviting tremor, and the romantic limp.[1]

Köhler was our first lecturer in this subject, and opposite our portrait of Byron you will see a diagram

[1] In the lecture-room where we teach limpmanship and the use of the silver-headed cane, there is a large oil painting of Byron to remind us that the present decay of Sir Walter Scott's reputation is in no small measure due to the fact that although Scott's limp was just as bad and just as genuine as Byron's, nobody ever heard about it. The Walter Scott picture was removed from the walls.

of the human figure crossed by a wavy line, known as "Köhler's Line." Köhler, originally a systematic botanist, attempted to standardise what he called "O.K. complaints" for various walks of life, above the line being in general more O.K. than below the line, though this varied interestingly, as can be imagined, in the case of such contrasted pursuits as those of poet, plasterer, racing driver, and diplomat, to name a few.

Odoreida-ism was rife in the early days of healthmanship—with Odoreida's irritating "You're looking remarkably fit" to Gattling just after he'd been thrown over by Claudia; or his "You're looking a bit cheap" to Cogg just after he'd been trying desperately to brown himself for ten dangerous days in the Engadine. In general I believe we have inculcated in our young Lifeman the rule that one must be able clearly to suggest either that one is absolutely healthy or, alternatively, never, really, free from pain. The two styles MUST NOT BE MUDDLED. On this basis all good health work must be grounded.[2]

Natural One-upness of Doctors.

But the first real hurdle to be tackled by the novice Healthman, when he comes of age, is the Doctor.

[2] An effective statement in the right context can sometimes be: "I have had 140 days' illness in my life." Listeners are unable, without a lame pause for calculation, to know whether to commiserate or admire.

We Lifemen have always been well disposed towards doctors. Above all professions, except perhaps that of the expert in commercial law, the Box Office manager, and the man whose special job it is to advise people about having their cars decarbonised, doctors have shown themselves to be apt and natural Lifemen, and their careers are built on a well-sprung framework of ploys and gambiting.

As some readers will not know, there is a *Lancet* [3] Research Group, denominating and codifying procedures. They have defined "Doctorship," with a rough directness, as the "art of getting one up on the patient without actually killing him." [4] Yes, but doctors, it must be remembered, are subjected to the healthy rivalry of Lifemanship from the very beginning of their training; and almost as soon as they are qualified they must decide (see *Lancet* Research) on whether to become one of four basic Doctor types.

Type One is the Damn-good-doctor, on the spot, enthusiastic, breathing common-sense, fond of simple remedies, and opposed to *Type Two,* the Damn-good-scientist. Damn-good-scientist prides himself on having "forgotten the starting symptoms of chicken-pox." He "hasn't listened to a chest since his Finals year."

[3] *Lancet.* The official organ of British Medicine, and recognised by us.

[4] "Nursemanship," the art of getting one up on the doctor and/or the patient without actually marrying either, is also described, with subsidiary anti-Sister ploys and contra-Matron gambits.

His clothes are stained with chemicals. The bulge in his pocket is graph-paper, not a stethoscope.[5]

A rarer but effective type is (*Three*) the man, continuously being caught out of reach of normal hospital equipment,[6] who learnt his Infectious Diseases in the stagnant marshes of the Naquipl foothills, where he was the only doctor in 15,000 square miles, if that. Finally there is (*Four*) the doctor who achieves eminence by always replying to the simplest possible question (after the smallest conceivable pause), "Alas, we don't know."

DOCTORSHIP: CROFT'S LAW OF INVERSE SUPERFICIAL DIFFERENTIATION IN TERMS OF MEAN EVOLUTIONARY ADDRESS

Reading from left to right, correct clothes for (1) 6a Verlaine Road, Portsea, Hants.; (2) "Fordingbridge," Dunting Road, Basingstoke; (3) 16 Redcliffe Gardens, Kensington; (4) 14 Wimpole Street, W.1; (5) President of the Royal College of Physicians.

[5] Additional *Lancet*-sponsored properties include a corked testtube of soapy water in the waistcoat pocket, a tuft of guinea-pig fur on the lapel, and the use of odd bits of cardiac catheter, instead of string, to tie things up with.

[6] St. Kildaship.

These types, potentially one up as each of them is, can be perpetually at war in the age-old struggle for the Survival of the Lifest. It is always the doctor who knows best how to appear to possess a better car than his nearest rival. The doctor who knows how to be one up in consulting-room equipment and clothes. (For our suggested diagonalising of clothes in relation to mean fashionable address, the top hat in the outer suburbs and the old fishing jacket for Harley Street, with gradations between, *see* Illustration.)

Natural One-downness of Patient.

What chance, it may well be asked, has even the lay Lifeman against the Doctor? The Doctor holds all the cards, and can choose his own way of playing them. Right at the start, when answering Patient's original phone call, for instance, he can, and generally does, say, "Dr. Meadows speaking," in a frightfully hollow and echoing voice, as if he was expecting a summons to sign a death certificate. Alternatively, a paralysingly brisk voice can be used suggesting that Doctor is busier than Patient in normal life, and in a more important way.

DOCTOR: Hallo, yes. Finchingfield here . . . Well, it will have to be rather late this morning. I'll see what I can do.

In the bedroom, the Irish type of M.D.man is tidier, better, or at any rate more crisply dressed than the Patient, and is able to suggest by his manner not only that Patient's room is surprisingly disordered, but that he, the Doctor, goes in for a more up-to-date type of pajamas than the ones he observes Patient to be wearing.

The Patient starts perkily enough:

LAYMAN: Thank you, doctor. I was coming home rather late last night from the House of Commons . . .

M.D.MAN: Thank you . . . now if you'll just let me put these . . . hair brushes and things off the bed for you . . . that's right . . .

LAYMAN: I was coming home rather late. Army Act, really—

M.D.MAN: Now just undo the top button of your shirt or whatever it is you're wearing . . .

LAYMAN: I say I was coming . . .

M.D.MAN: Now if you've got some hot water—really hot—and a clean towel.

LAYMAN: Yes, just outside. The Postmaster-General . . .

M.D.MAN: Open your mouth please.

To increase the one-downness, bring in the washing-the-hands gambit immediately after touching hands with Patient. Unpleasant infectant possibilities can be suggested.

The old, now discarded, bedside mannership is still used when Doctor wishes to subdue the sensitive patient suffering from an eclipsing headache. Doctor used to begin a constant fire of hollowly exploding clubroom stories, so involved in their climax that only the keenest attention revealed the point of expected laughter. We now teach that the M.D.man should show an *inaccurate familiarity with the patient's own tastes or profession.* He can suggest, for instance, that some prized first edition "might be worth something some day," or, if his patient is a horseman, tell him that the first syllable in "Pytchley" is long. For actor-patients, Doctor can tell the story of how as a young student he dressed up as Principal Boy in the Middlesex Hospital Pantomime when a member of the Middlesex Mauve Merriments.

After this opening treatment, Doctor may, *under certain circumstances,* ask Patient his symptoms. But he will let it be seen that he is not listening to what Patient is saying, and may place his hand on Patient's wrist, or, better, stomach, as if to suggest that he as Doctor can tell more through the sensitive tip of one finger than from listening to the layman's self-deceiving, ill-observed, and hysterically redundant *impressions* of what is wrong with him.

Many good M.D.men make a point of shepherding

their patients into the consulting room where, by his way of averting his head as Patient is undressing, Doctor can suggest criticism of his choice of underclothes, socks, &c. The doctor is well. You are longing for a cigarette. And you are ill. And in more ways than in mere physical health.

Nevertheless the following Friendly Consulting Room Approach [7] is basically better. Suppose your patient comes in with, say, a chronic outbreak of warts on the back of the neck. He will be disposed to make light of this. ALLOW HIM TO, BUT FRIGHTEN HIM AT THE SAME TIME, by little asides to invisible nurses. Thus:

M.D.MAN: Well, you are a pretty sight. Now, just lower your shirt.

LAYMAN: (*enjoying himself*): Not very pretty for sunbathing at Annecy next summer. I thought . . .

M.D.MAN: Better take it right off. Ah, you lucky man. You know the lake, do you? (*Lowering voice*) Nurse, get me a Watson-Dunn, will you?

LAYMAN: Yes, I love it, we go every year . . .

M.D.MAN (*pressing buzzer*): The food of course is marvellous. (*Speaking calmly into some machine*)

---

[7] This gambit was invented by a well-known actor, with medical tastes. Shunning publicity, he yet allows me to say that it was evolved in Rome during the filming of *Quo Vadis*. He was in charge of the St. John's Ambulance Tent, block L, during the scenes when the lions were eating the Christians—largely faked. He himself was playing the part of the Emperor Ustinian.

Oh Barker, get me the light syringe from the steriliser—yes, the dual. Yes, we must get you right for that.

LAYMAN: But it's not anything . . .

M.D.MAN: Nothing serious, I'm sure. Now bend down. Yes, Annecy—and you know Talloires? . . . Now nurse, if you'll just stand by while we have a look. Quadriceps please . . . and—oh, thank you,

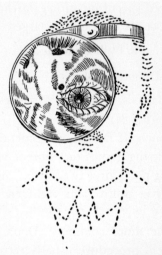

DR. J. HOLLIS CARTER'S EEZISLIPON

This "speculum" is fitted with coated lenses which flash in the eye of the perturbed patient a magnified portion of doctor's face upside down.

"Sign manual of the well-run clinic."
Scotsman

"Induces Cheyne-Stokes respiration and a Watts-Dunton anxiety."
Lancet

Barker. Better get the hydrogeniser going (*compressed air sound can be imitated by some assistant in the background going "zzzz" through his teeth*). Yes, there's a little restaurant—right down please—the Georges Bise . . . Now.

At the end, with a charming "au revoir," M.D.man, instead of telling him what is wrong, can stare, last thing, at frightened Patient's left eye through a specially contrived speculum which startles Patient with a view of Doctor's own eye, enlarged, inverted, and bloodshot (*see* Illustration).

Some Slight Discomfortship.

Doctorship Basic is, of course, to suggest that Patient is worrying either (a) too little, but (b) far more generally, too much. If (a), a good general suggestion is that he is playing games too violent for his time of life. "No ping-pong after twenty-six," he will say. Or, "After fifty-five, more than eighteen holes is . . . well . . ."

But for the more common "Don't make such a fuss" approach, procedure usually recommended for M.D.men is as follows:

1. If patient has rash, describe some really serious skin disease seen in hospital that morning, as if this mentioning of a few silly spots was futile.

2. For stiff neck, put on an obviously assumed interest, say "I'm sorry to hear of that," and if Patient says

he has been awakened six times during the night by really sharp twinges, be overheard saying to some assistant that "Patient appears to have had some slight discomfort. I shall not be in to lunch to-day." [8]

3. When treating a cold, Doctor can go rather mechanically through a list of prescriptions, remedies, and a routine which the patient "must" follow, and then say, "I've got just the same sort of cold myself, they're about everywhere. What do *I* do about it? Well, personally I do nothing whatever. Absolutely nothing, I'm sorry to say. Just go on as if nothing had happened. What? Bed, that is my orders to you." All the time, Doctor is suggesting that his constitution, character, inherited resistance, courage, and will-power is in every way stronger than Patient's.

Gambit 4 is for Patient who wants to be made a fuss of. His warts are painful. His neck is swollen. Make him feel a fool by writing down everything he says.

M.D.MAN: When did you first notice all this?

LAYMAN: My neck began to get a bit red—end of month.

M.D.MAN (*writing*): "End of month . . . neck becomes red . . ."

LAYMAN: They didn't really hurt till last week.

M.D.MAN: "After eighteen days . . . some discomfort." Yes. This is the eighth case of false warts I've seen this week.

[8] Gattling-Fenn tells me that just after the birth of his son, the monthly nurse was constantly overheard by his wife Mou-mou (then feeling particularly low) giving news to telephone enquirers that "We're all doing splendidly. Mother is feeling wonderfully fit."

LAYMAN: What do you mean, false?

M.D.MAN: Only the root is involved.

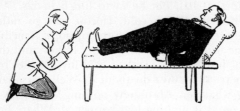

M.D.MANSHIP

A simple method of making patient feel a fool. If he complains of earache after bathing, examine his plantar surfaces.

Modern Methodship.

Many Doctors, of course, use Modern Methodship, which consists in irritating or upsetting the patient by the totally irrelevant diagnostic approach. E.g., in comes the man with warts. M.D.man takes one glance at the warts and then asks him to lie down.

M.D.MAN: Right. Relax. Now when did you first notice the warts?

LAYMAN: Oh, about—months ago.

M.D.MAN: Right. Now try lifting the right leg slowly . . . down . . . now turn the foot sharply to the left—no, *left*. Now sit up. Up. Do you ever relax?

LAYMAN: Oh—*yes*.

M.D.MAN: No—I mean every muscle, cheeks, nose—gums . . .

27

The Totally Irrelevant Question can be brought in here. This is sometimes known as Allergyship.

M.D.MAN: Tell me, what sort of nail varnish does your wife use?

LAYMAN (*beginning to get sour*): Not married.

M.D.MAN: Not? Do you keep chickens under your bedroom window?

LAYMAN: Sloane Avenue Mansions doesn't encourage chickens.

M.D.MAN: Of course not. Look, now, do you mind if I have a look at your fountain pen? Yes. Thanks. Yes.

Opposed to this is:

Traditional Methodship.

Traditional Methodship consists in blurting out every now and then something about "what she wants isn't psycho-howsit or even deep-ray thingummy but a good slap on the whatsisname." If Patient turns out to be really ill after all, it is always possible to look grave and proud at the same time, and say, "You realise, I suppose, that 25 years ago you'd have been dead?" [9]

[9] We are working at the moment on a new and somewhat contrasted technique of alarming patients, which we call the Factor of Uncertain Trust. In its present rough state we keep it to a footnote. The doctor adopts a man-to-man attitude, and admits right away that he is not quite sure. To give the wording advised by our visiting Welbeck Demonstrator, C. Hobbs:
M.D.MAN: Let's have a look at these warts. (*Begins to whistle a slow*

The Need for Organised Patientship.

It will be seen that the whole doctor/patient situation bristles with difficulties for the layman. But is it not precisely this kind of problem—this apparently fixed one-upness of doctors—which we of L.C.C. like best to tackle?

In homely language, how can the Patient get back?

Divers approaches to the problem were attempted in the early days, only to be discarded. It used to be thought that it would curb the Doctor's high spirits to be asked if, after diagnosing mumps, he "would mind bringing in another opinion." But it was soon discovered that the doctor's solemn expression concealed a delight in being able to get an extra fee for poor old Pettinglass.

---

tune) They *are* warts, are they? But isn't there something that looks rather like a wart which you have to take out, or something? Wait a minute—where's my book? Where's Price—big red—here it is. Funny, they haven't got anything about warts in the index. Some long-winded medical word, I suppose . . . here's something. Oh yes, it says: "Inject with novo-phosthene." Do you mind if I just look that up? Little grey book somewhere. No, I haven't got novo-phosthene, but I've got something damned like it. Damned like it. Now, we're supposed to use a squee-gee. Oh Lord, I haven't used one of those things for years. Supposed to put it under the tap. All these "do's" and "don't's." Now then . . . Now look, you're going to help me. If you'd just mind pushing . . . (*begins a jolly laugh*) Go on, push against it! Push!

A refinement on this gambit has just been received from Ireland. If Price is missing from the Doctor's shelf, as it probably will be, let him take down a book titled in large letters *Veterinary Surgery*. Or, better still, R. Casey suggests *A Simple Manual for Dog Lovers*.

Some success is reported from married couples who have trained their youngest child to say in a clear voice, "Mummy, I don't like that man" whenever a doctor comes into the room. This is now not much used.

Marvellous Little Manship.

This is a proved doctor-irritant, especially if the ploy is executed by a well-dressed woman patient visiting Harley Street address of physician holding dignified position at London Hospital who is one who prides himself particularly on never being guilty of Harleyship *per se*.

Recommended dialogue runs as follows:

LIFEWOMAN: I was wondering whether that marvellous little man in Curzon Street would be able to help me, doctor?

HARLEYMAN: Oh yes? What little man?

LIFEWOMAN: Olaf Pepacanek. *How* do you pronounce it?

HARLEYMAN: I'm afraid I've never heard of him.

LIFEWOMAN: Oh, but he's a most marvellous man— he *weighs* everything. He says that English doctors don't realise that what he calls the square foods and the round foods can cancel each other out. He's written a book.

HARLEYMAN: Oh yes.

LIFEWOMAN: It's called *Bricks Without Straw*.
HARLEYMAN: Oh yes.

This is often quite irritating. Our Wimpole Reader, Gattling-Fenn, is working on what he calls rather long-windedly the Patient's Deskside Manner counter to the Doctor's Bedside Approach. In the consulting room, the doctor is tapping Gattling's chest. Gattling exudes a confident cheerfulness.

DOCTOR: (*Taps*)
GATTLING: Tap away.
DOCTOR: Now the back.
GATTLING: Thorough is as thorough does. You chaps certainly put us through the hoop nowadays.
DOCTOR: 99.
GATTLING: Dial 999, eh? (*Sings*) I'm 99 to-day, I'm 99 to-day.
DOCTOR: Keep still, please.
GATTLING: Still as a mouse.
DOCTOR: Quiet.
GATTLING (*Pause, begins to laugh*): I suppose it's all necessary but my great-uncle was a bit of a sawbones. Doctors were doctors in those days. Anyhow I know HE was able to take his old wooden stethoscope and diagnose lobar pneumonia through two woollen vests and a horse-hair overcoat in thirty seconds dead.[10]

[10] *Lancet*-sponsored phrasing.

Under examination, Gattling would counter the danger of nudeship ("the natural one-downness of the unclothed" [11]) by arranging telephone calls direct to the consulting room carefully timed to coincide with the maximum unclothed condition. He had himself

rung by an aristocratically confident female voice and would then become involved in a long conversation, obviously with some wealthy and attractive girl, and burst out twice into long telephone laughter, slapping his bare thigh and shouting: "This is colossal! Tell me more!"

Further minor counter-doctor ploys are:

[11] Many will recognise this as the phrase inscribed under the dome of the Hunterian amphitheatre at St. George's.

GMCmanship.

This is defined as the "playing on the doctor's fears of seeming to seek either publicity or kudos for medical qualifications which in fact he does not possess."

It is possible to throw doubt on the very term doctor—"I am, I suppose, right in calling you 'doctor'?" Again, if the doctor asks, "Don't you think your symptoms have a psychological basis?" (always a weak ploy), reply at once, "I had no idea that was one of your subjects. I have always wanted a good psychotherapist." Refuse to take in his worried assurance that he is not a trained psychiatrist. You "will tell your friends" about him.

Under this same heading, if Doctor tells Patient that he has been spending the week-end in deepest Bucks where he saw, say, Bob Hope and his niece, Patient can reply: "Hope told me, and—surprise for you!—that snap Babette took of you and Bob joking together with a stethoscope in the bathing-pool is being published in the *Tatler*."

In contrast with this there is:

Title Ploy.

This consists of annoying your personal consultant by pretending to think that all doctors like titled patients. Talk in what is called the Titles Voice about your friend Geoffrey Dunn who has just been flown over to Dublin to have a look at the Marquis Conne-mara's little girl and her tiresome attack of thrush. Even if this does not irritate your doctor it will certainly get him off beat. Some Lifemen add, "I must see if I can get you one or two little plums like that."

Certain patients, especially at Christmas time or on other festive occasions, go to extraordinary lengths to make the doctor feel awkward after a consulting-room examination. When redressing, for instance, they will roll their collar-stud under the doctor's couch, grope for it, and appear to "find" either a small medicine bottle half-full of crème de menthe, or a set of false teeth embedded in a meringue.[12] It only remains to ask "Are these yours?" in a plonking tone of voice, and the usual results follow.

Specialist Counter Lifepatient Play.

An intensely effective ploy often used by M.D.men but overlooked in their published researches is for Doctor to treat Patient not only as if he knew nothing about medicine but as if Patient were as ignorant of all anatomical knowledge as a child of four. Often M.D.man will give totally unnecessary technical names and then explain them—e.g., "that mild rhinitis of yours: sniffles to you." Or to a Lifepatient particularly anxious to show off his knowledge, he will talk like this:

[12] Both supplied by Lifemanship Accessories, Ltd.

LIFEPATIENT (*knowledging*): I came to you because trivial as the condition looks there was this distinct oedoematous area under the warts.

M.D.MAN: Yes, it is a bit puffy. Tell me, does it go *Pong*-Pong, *Pong*-Pong?

LIFEPATIENT: You mean does it throb? Are the growths vascular?

M.D.MAN: Now don't you worry about that. You see, the heart is a sort of pump . . .

LIFEPATIENT: Yes—please—but . . .

M.D.MAN: It goes squeez-o, squeez-o—no, look at my hand.

LIFEPATIENT: I am, but . . .

M.D.MAN: And the blood isn't just blood, it's full of little soldiers, all fighting against each other.

LIFEPATIENT: Yes.

M.D.MAN: Have you ever been in the Army?

LIFEPATIENT: Well, no, but . . .

M.D.MAN: You've heard the word "corpuscles." Now both those are the white fellows and the red chaps. Now this is how the battle begins. At the source of the infection—where Something's Wrong . . .

Even experienced Lifepatients can be silenced in the end by this treatment. Easier to deal with is that dangerous Harleyman who tries to put you in your place when you go to him for a stiff neck by suggesting that you are being rather trivial and he is feeling rather tired—up all night transfusing a couple of touch-and-go cases of thrombocytopenic purpura. It is always possible for Lifepatient to reply: "I'm sorry to have bothered you with this apparently trivial thing, but my friend Eddie Webb-Johnson [13] persuaded me to go to a really competent general physician if I could find one. He prodded me about for twenty minutes or so and told me to let him know the results of a more careful examination; and who was doing it, what were his qualifications, and so on.

"By the way—just to stop him bothering—what are your qualifications?"

[13] Lord Webb-Johnson is the most O.K. surgical name in Britain.

III

Businessmanship

1. THE PROBLEM

YEOVIL'S SCHOOL of Businessmanship is not yet fully formed. It is a strange fact, which we here state in all frankness and without criticism, that vast as are its resources the business world has made small contribution to our funds. "We invented Lifemanship before you were born," said a bulk buyer of synthetic soup by-products to me the other day, and this conveys the attitude of the whole business community. "Certainly," said his friend, who disposed of the residue of the soup by-products, which he patented as compressed fuel. "And didn't we invent the word Salesmanship?"

"Yes, and Chairmanship too," said a heavy-jowled older man, who bought up the remains of the residue of this soup by-product for his firm, Natural Broths, Ltd.

And of course one must sympathise with this view. "Businessmanship—Salesmanship—Lifemanship" . . . and yet. At any rate when the concrete request came for guidance, a request from the business quarter of New York City, we were glad to add this youngest of all our student courses to our schedule.

Lifemanship's Principle of Negative Selling.

What is our approach? On the wall of Commercial Corner, in the East Wing of our College, there hangs

BUSINESSMANSHIP BASIC

"It's men like you we want."
Alternatively
"It's men like me you want."

a picture. It is taken from the wrapper of a popular American Salesmanship Manual. (Note to Illustrator: reproduce *picture only* on the cover of *Sizzlemanship* by Elmer Wheeler.) Look at the picture. On the left is a figure full of the confidence of the man who knows his job and knows it is well done. The Salesman. On the right is the prospective client, the "Prospect," his eagerness to buy only matched by his astonished admiration of this fine and courageous personality who is forcing him into a deal which his reason abhors. That is the implied interpretation.

There you have the business of Business. But in Businessmanship the roles must be reversed. The sitting figure on the *right* is the salesman, trained by us in that bungling diffidence which alone can infuse confidence into the buyer and fill him with certainty that this feeble sap before him couldn't deceive a milk pudding.[1]

The No-pen Approach.

For our first simple lesson we demonstrate the basic gambit of the No-pen Approach—easy phrase to re-

---

[1] This is the only picture in our Business lecture-room because it can be used to illustrate the right and wrong methods of Salesmanship and anything else as well. E.g., I am sometimes asked is there a Lifeman's put-off for insurance salesman. Yes, there is, and this picture demonstrates it. In Method One, the "Prospect" (left) is countering the insurance salesman (right) by a sudden stream of praise for insurance policies in general and a suggestion, since the salesman earns his living by talking, that he should insure either (a) his hard palate or (b) his right fist, essential in forceful speech and especially liable to accident. In Method Two, Prospect (right) is asking salesman (left) if he would mind continuing the conversation at home, take pot-luck with his aunts, and give a comic recitation to help entertain the displaced children of the Paper-cutters' Orphanage—"they're quite all right if you know how to handle them, and we ought to be back before 1 A.M."

member. Childishly primary, it yet embodies the Lifemanship's Principle of Negative Selling.

Lay businessmen when they are anxious—typical business problem—to persuade a client to sign some document containing a clause which on closer inspection will be seen to the client's disadvantage, sometimes do it like this. With the document on the desk, the dialogue is as follows:

LAY BUSINESSMAN: I think you'll find everything quite in order, Mr. Fortinbras.

FORTINBRAS: Oh yes, but what about the—

L.B. (*oiling in*): You did want us to keep mutually independent? Now, you sit here.

FORTINBRAS (*puzzled*): Something about "giving you right of transference"?

L.B.: That's right.

FORTINBRAS (*suspicious*): Yes, but—

L.B.: Now, if you just put your name where I pencilled it in. I think you'll find my pen in working order . . .

What is wrong? The untrained businessman is standing ready with gleaming fountain pen full of rich ink. He is hovering. He is amiable. Client is put on the defensive and ten to one he will begin to ask questions.

Study now the Lifemanship-trained Businessman in the same position. Once more, the document is on the table, all ready for Mr. Fortinbras.

BUSINESS LIFEMAN: I think this is the thing you're supposed to sign.

MR. FORTINBRAS: I beg your pardon?

B.L.: Only for goodness' sake let's make sure. Must get my secretary to tidy my desk.

F. (*amused*): Well, here's my name, anyhow.

B.L.: Let's try and take it in. (*Reading very slowly*.) "Whereas the party hereinafter called the copy-holders shall within the discretion of both signatories"—can't understand a word.

F. (*almost paternal already*): Let me. I'm used to this sort of jargon. "The parties assigned . . ."

B.L.: Look. Wonderful, isn't it? (*They laugh*.)

F. (*taking charge*): That's right, and I'm supposed to sign there—paragraphs individually, aren't I?

B.L.: Oh? I mean *yes*. Awfully sorry, don't seem to have a pen (*rustles through papers*). I'm most awfully sorry, I've got a new secretary. Josephine! Probably at coffee. Typical.

F.: It's all right, I've got a pen.

B.L. (*keen for the first time*): Oh, isn't that the new sort that writes on ice, or something? Marvellous little thing. Can I look at it? Sorry, after you.

41

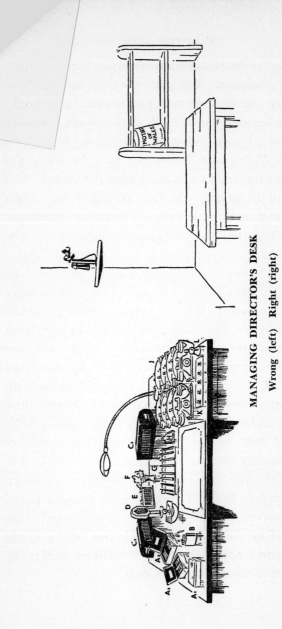

MANAGING DIRECTOR'S DESK

Wrong (left) Right (right)

"Sorry," because client is already in the act of signing the document. The client is helping. To make assurance doubly sure in this technique, it is no bad thing if businessman actually puts client's borrowed pen into his own pocket, after admiring it, as if by mistake. Client now leaves, not only having signed the paper but full of a queer sort of confidence. This signature technique was first perfected by Lumer Farr, and it is known as Lumer's Bumbling Approach.

This negative fountain-penmanship sets the note of our course. We teach students to remember that it is only men *below* the highest rank in any firm who take exact measurements of the carpet in their office room to make sure it is not narrower than Y's or less thick than Z's. But in Supreme Boss-ship we always teach plainness, simplicity, and downright ordinariness. No Yeovil-trained managing director ever dreams of being seen behind a desk clanking with telephones, loud speakers, soft speakers, buzzers, little flashing lights, and silver boxes overflowing with splendid cigarettes and engraved with the signatures of supposedly affectionate colleagues. No. Take Lumer Farr, Yeovil-trained Vice-President (lifeword for Complete Boss) of International Packing Cases. "You'd never think," I have heard people say, "that Lumer Farr controlled three-quarters of the crude teak export trade of Canada." Actually he didn't, but why should anyone think he did?

Lumer likes to be called "The Guv'nor," but likes it to be thought that he likes to be called "Bert." [2] His nose is a thin beak, but his eyes and chin are faint and ghostly, neither commanding nor firm. He creeps about in a little black coat. His desk is a plain deal table with nothing on it whatever. The only telephone in the room is an old-fashioned candlestick one in the corner with a winder. He gets up and answers it himself about twice during the morning. Guarding his room of course there are ranks and ranks of fashionable men and women dressed as secretaries, whose function it is to be extremely busy and to keep anybody except some ne'er-do-well nephew [3] from ringing up or speaking to Lumer. These rebuffs in which he has trained this group are delightfully contrasted with Lumer's occasional bemused and affable appearances at the doorway of his office when he may ask you himself to come in, and apologises for the lack of courtesy with which you have been treated.

---

[2] In the science of Christian-naming, Lumer is associated with Farr's Law of Mean Familiarity. This can be expressed by a curve, but is much clearer set down as follows:

The Guv'nor addresses:

Co-director Michael Yates as	MIKE
Assistant director Michael Yates as	MICHAEL
Sectional manager Michael Yates as	MR. YATES
Sectional assistant Michael Yates as	YATES
Apprentice Michael Yates as	MICHAEL
Night-watchman Michael Yates as	MIKE

[3] Lumer's "Ploy of the Ridiculously Soft Heart." He always says, "Suppose I'd better speak to the young scallywag." But he has never actually given him either help or money.

44

Then he will fumble out a broken packet and offer you a twisted cigarette.

Lumer is always slipping out of the room and slipping into the room in a way which is supposed to be unnoticed but which in fact everybody is supposed to notice. When he gets out of a car or a plane or even coming out of the theatre, he will slip quietly away, head down, as if he were avoiding a reporter. And quite late at night he will be seen, by arrangement, alone at this empty desk, on the plain deal chair.

2. COMMITTEESHIP

I have enunciated a general principle: let me now outline the work of one of our study circles, Committeeship.

It is axiomatic that Committeeship is the art of coming into a discussion without actually understanding a word of what anybody is talking about. But this entry can be made effective only if the speaker *decides what sort of person he, the speaker, is, and sticks to it*. The sort doesn't much matter, consistency is what counts; but the following committeeship types are especially recommended:

Type One, MULSIPRAT. The man who, pretty high and perhaps chairman, is yet rather muddled. At the same time he is never in a flap about his mistakes but says "There I go again" or "There's another of my beauts." [4] This is endearing and in fact the point of Mulsiprat is being adored by everybody. He may employ two special secretaries, one male and one female, whose exclusive difficult duty is to [5] obviously adore him.

Type Two, GALEAD, is also rather mad. But this rathermadmanship is of a totally different sort. Galead is manic, never cuts nails, has one shoe-lace undone, wears new jackets *with one button missing,* reveals faint tremor of the left hand, chain-smokes (dummy nicotine stains may be varnished onto the backs of the fingers). He sometimes adds to this a speech-disability-sign—e.g., starting every remark with a long downward cadence whistle—it (*whistle*) "cures my stammer."

In committee he is the permanently "difficult" one: "(*Whistle*) Yes, but *how?*" Early in the meeting he finds himself in definite disagreement with the Chairman and Managing Director on some minor issue, which makes it all the easier for him to be overwhelmingly on their side round about lunch time.

Type Three, LUDLOW, is the tremendously ordinary chap valuable because he is in close touch with tremendously ordinary people and can, himself,

[4] The wording here and certain other ploys in this section were hacked out in committee with a dissatisfied group of low-ranking members of the editorial staff of *Fortune.*

[5] For our life-sponsored split infinitive, see our next publication, *Womanship,* 1954.

talk tremendously ordinarily.[6] We can't do without Ludlow because he is the man in the street.

DIAGRAM OF MAN IN THE STREET

Type Four, MAIDENHAIR, we draw special attention to because he represents a totally new type, of

DIAGRAM OF MAN NOT IN THE STREET (Drawn to reduced scale.)

[6] Not to be confused with the man who talks tremendously ordinarily to children. *See Lifemanship,* Chap. One.

high value, as we believe, and something we are perhaps rather specially proud of because he has been developed entirely through Lifemanship-sponsored organisations. He is the man not in the street. Sometimes, he has taken a First in Classics, and is often therefore brilliant.

Type Five, TEMPESTRIAN, is not brilliant at all but sensible. He counters suggestions of brilliant Type Maidenhair by saying, "Yes, but don't let's forget the big picture. What, after all, are we trying to do?"

Type Six, CO-AX, is in a way wicked, or at any rate puts business first and says so. In the world of journalism, he is so hard-boiled about tender feelings that rival committeemen are thought to feel awe. His voice is thin and waxy. "What we want on this page here," he says, "is a picture of a displaced crippled sick orphan of exiled alien parents and plug it for all we're worth." One day we were discussing the insertion of a rather daring portrait of fairly pretty Paulette O. in our little mag. "Page Three," Co-Ax said, hard-boiling. "We want sex on page three, nine inches by eight. Always assuming that we have a story about cruelty to animals on page seven." This always goes down particularly well with the shyer shareholders who may be fairly strong family men and church-wardens. "Co-Ax knows his job," they say afterwards, downing their small gin-and-limes in one.

Type Seven, HOSPITER, can be any of the foregoing, and yet none. He is the natural counter-committeeman, the underminer. It is not what he is, but what he says, that matters.

Hospiter Parlettes, many of them silent, are as follows:

(a) When rival committeeman is speaking.

i. Look sadly at boots (it is best to have actual boots).

ii. Doodle and continue to doodle with the faintest possible deepening of the corners of the mouth. Try to suggest that you see something irresistibly inappropriate or comic in what your rival is saying, but wild horses wouldn't make you spoil his little speech by mentioning it now. This delicate and highly expert little ploy was first described to me independently by H. Whyte and F. Anderson, and named by the latter the "Mona Lisa Ploy."

(b) When rival committeeman has finished speaking, say:

i. "Well, we sort of came to a decision about that, didn't we, after a fairly full discussion last week, a rather good discussion, I thought. I mean we agree."

Or alternatively say:

ii. "Well," (*pause and look hard at chairman as if only you two know this*) "there are definite reasons why that is going to become impracticable fairly shortly, aren't there?"

Or say:

iii. "Yes, but we have got to think of the effect on the ordinary nice people we meet in the street. They are not terribly brainy but they are quite nice people really."

49

If rival makes obviously good bold and original point, counter it by saying:

i. "Yes, I think that's a good idea—I wonder if we were right to discard it five years ago when there was all that row."

Or:

ii. if you can only think of something conventional and commonplace as alternative, *make* your flat suggestion in an "Of course I'm completely mad" voice (*flairship*), and add "I know you'll think I'm making a fool of myself, but I think some of us are bound to make fools of ourselves before anything really happens, don't you?"

Or:

iii. simply say, "Yes, but that isn't really what we're discussing, is it?"

Regil and the Economics Ploy.

Type Eight, REGIL,[7] is different from all the foregoing if only because he knows if possible less about the subject under discussion, and the business of the committee generally, than anybody else present. He is rather like Maidenhair, the first in classics, except that the general impression is that Regil took a first in economics.

Regil invariably creates an economics wicket by referring everything to the social or monetary sciences.

[7] These titles may have some religious or cosmographical significance, or they may be the names of the first eight losers backed by us in the Yeovil Handicap, Spring, 1952.

He often speaks of "structured behaviour" and uses the phrase "inner directed," frequently mixing it, according to Whyte of Manhattan, with a colloquialism ("He's pretty much of an inner-directed guy.").

Regil however certainly comes into his best on his own subject, economics—"the plonking science," as Matthew Arnold called it; and it is generally agreed that almost any phrase from any chapter of this extraordinary subject will meet any emergency, if the sentences are spelt out sufficiently slowly and clearly.

Sometimes, of course, Regil, especially after a short snifter, enjoyed himself with a little wild incomprehensibility (Economics Approach A).

"If you want to influence the general liquidity situation of banks *and* public," he would say, pretending to expect a reply. "If you do," he would go on, "I think you're forgetting that the Bank of England's discretionary action on the cash basis took the shape of dealings in Treasury Bills, the market rate of discount on which could *and did* fluctuate."

Regil would firm up his voice a good deal on "did fluctuate." But he was always at his best I thought on the more classical *Economics Approach B,* (the "Approach of Utter Obviousness").

This "stupefaction of the exhaustingly clear" (Watertower) was used by Regil at moments of some crisis. "I'm not going to tell you why most demand curves slope downward," he would begin, as a paralyser. Then he would become clear, in that frightful way of his. "Unless something happens to change the state of demand," he would say, as if he was quoting and incredibly enough he was, "more will be bought at any given price than at any higher price."

Another pause, before the next sentence, when his voice became so cuttingly audible it seemed to pass straight to the centre of my head and shortcut the organs of comprehension completely: "Any rise in price WILL REDUCE THE VOLUME OF SALES."

Suddenly he was quiet again, for the homely instance:

"When a child enters a shop to buy a pennorth of sourballs, *by the mere fact of asking for the sourballs it incurs a debt of one penny.* Look . . ."

I knew this "look" of Regil's. It was the prelude to a sort of Economics Oration, which we were all too hypnotised to interrupt:

"Look, and what do you see?"
Generally I saw the ash-tray, steaming with unfinished cigarettes.
"You see the farm labourer in the fields, tending the cattle to be marketed. The factory workers controlling the machines, feeding them with raw materials which they *transform into manufactured produce.* The miner is extracting mineral deposits from the earth, the clerk is recording transactions in the office, transport workers are moving persons and goods from one place to another. By cable and wireless, instructions are transmitted with amazing speed . . ."

And so it went on. The fact that most of us were always complaining of telephone delays, and that none of us had ever actually seen any of these things (except perhaps Rusper the clerk) didn't stop Regil from having another of his recurrent successes, from flattening the committee into respectful silence, and from mounting, with one foot on "produce" and another on "goods," yet one more rung on Businessmanship's difficult ladder.

IV

The Correspondence College Department of Artistic Practice

THE COMPLETE PRINTED syllabus of our courses is available through the usual channels, but, as the two Schools I have so far described are both vocational, I am anxious to reassure readers that the Arts are not neglected at Yeovil. On the contrary, I doubt whether there is any department in which new ground is more obviously broken.

The Doing of the Doing.

Whereas most Universities teach the function, history, practice, and criticism of drama, music, and the plastic arts, no attention whatever is given "to the doing of the doing"—i.e., to that natural one-upness which even the Lifeman visitor to theatre or concert can so unobtrusively suggest, and which the actual Life-artist, the creator, assumes as a natural right. How often do we not find, in the pre-Gameslifemanship era, that the artist is actually one down?

De-Slading and Counter RADAship.*

Painters, writers, and actors particularly find, to take one example, that our Corrective Course, for ex-students of the best establishments, is a blessing. "Opens a new world in a fortnight," wrote one.

Take a would-be writer who has just taken a First-Class Honours in English Language and Literature at Oxford—Balliol, typically. What chance has he got of success in an author's career compared, say, to a tramp, a lieutenant-general, or a photographer of East African animals.

Or take the RADAman—the dramatic student. He may have been trained and passed with Honours in basic movement including basic sitting-down, a silver medallist in basic door-shutting, basic speech, basic silence, and basic basic. But these accomplishments can scarcely be said to put him in the one-up position or make a Chapter Two for the theatrical autobiog-

* The Slade School of painting, and the Royal Academy of Dramatic Art, are respectively the most O.K. colleges for artists and actors in Britain.

raphy we generally recommend should be written at the age of twenty-four.

Humble Startship.

No. For genius-ship, a smooth beginning is fatal. In our Edmund Kean Wing we roughen these young people, we put them through a course of Crummle-ship. In the constant smell of grease-paint, sprayed through special nozzles powered by diesel fans, we let them mingle with the dust of a typical green-room (painted by the Brothers Harker). They learn to juggle, to walk the tight-rope, to wander about in the flies, to go without food for thirty-six hours, while they wait to fetch pints of beer for a drunken stage-manager who teaches them nothing except how to receive an oath and a cuff.[1] We teach the girls, while still in the dingy lodgings and unhealthy surroundings which we provide, to step at one hour's notice, still rubbing embrocation on bruises pitifully redolent of stout beer, into some performance of, say, Beatrice in *Much Ado* or Bridget in *While The*.[2] Between the acts they eat dummy steak and onions and drink a pint of porter, then go home to the wretched apartment of the travelling mummer. They may be RADA-

[1] The post of this "stage-manager" is filled (by Leonard Moppet of Buttermere).

[2] We encourage professionally abbreviated names of the plays of Shakespeare and Rattigan (*While the Sun Shines*). Actually, we shorten them even more, sometimes calling "Much Ado" "Much."

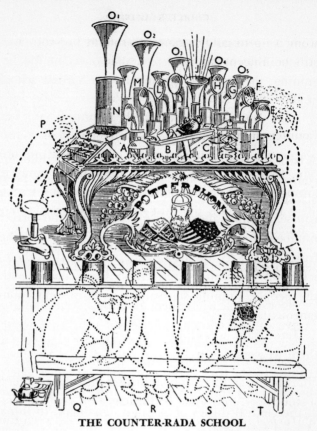

THE COUNTER-RADA SCHOOL

This drawing of the Potterphon, evolved for our Founder by F. Wilson, for teaching students to act the mad scene in *Hamlet* under conditions of mean average distraction, is self-explanatory. Students will note (A) bell for simulating fire engines passing down Shaftesbury Avenue; (B) tea-tray rattler; (C) paper-bag crumpler; (D) student-actors speaking the line "Here's rosemary, that's for remembrance"; (E) icy blast from wings; (F) dust from flies; (G) whiff of greasepaint; (H) whiff of beer; (J) tea attendants saying they haven't got change; (L) sweet-sucking; (M) orange-sucking, with whiff; (N) distant voice calling "Star News Standard"; (0 1-5) coughs, whispers, &c., controlled by mixer; (Q-T) inattentive audition-holders.

women up to golden goblet standards but they will still be able to say, and feel, that once, in the beginning, they were struggling in the hardest school of all.

Counter-Slading.

A basically similar though outwardly totally different course is given to young art students who have been Slading away for three years, admirably taught, of course, Antique and Life, who have spent the correct number of vacations in Paris and even enjoyed the fruits of a Prix de Rome, thereby shutting themselves off apparently irretrievably from contact with the people, humble startship, naïveship, and spontaneous folk art.

Here again we supply the humble start and set them to work locally, in the signal box at the level crossing by the back of our garden, for instance, where they have no time, labouring fourteen hours a day at the clerical duties of assistant-signalman, to think of easel and palette. Yet their art will begin to show itself in the decorations they will add, naïvely bold, painted on the gateposts of the level crossing, or in chalk drawings of village wedding scenes rubbed on the back of the routine reports of changes in the railway time-table or dossiers of local goods-trains. These we make a point of discovering after three months, whereupon, in little less than ten years, the new artist has slightly more chance of placing his work in Bond Street, or at any rate of being noticed in Park Crescent.

V

A Note on Exhibitionship¹

The following paragraphs were issued at the request of the Arts Council on the occasion of the opening of the South Bank Festival of Britain exhibition. We reprint them here unaltered.

"Exhibitionship" is the name for the various ploys and gambits connected with the art of being, or seeming to be, a visitor to an exhibition. It is not the art of exhibiting (Barryship).

The basic gambit is of course the achievement of the state of one-upness on the rest of the public. A word of advice then, perhaps particularly to the for-

¹ I am going to make no mention in this note of "Bonding," as it is miscalled, because this is dealt with in a special pamphlet Y.16, "Bonding for Beginners," which deals with what to say at the Redfern, what to say at the Lefevre, and what to say at the Leicester, and other Bond Street Galleries not in Bond Street.

eigner—always welcomed to our country by the lifeman—on certain simple methods of visiting an exhibition.

Classical Wrong Approach.

Though there are confusing exceptions to this rule,
British visitors to London go to exhibitions as a duty,
not a pleasure. Note at the zoo the fixed smile of the
mother, determined to get through with it good-hu-
moredly. Note, in the Egyptian Room of the British
Museum, how grim the father and how quivering
the elder sister. "Stand still, Frank," she says. Or,
"You'll spoil everything," to the seething child who is
visibly fermenting, having been fed on nothing but
starch since they all left Colchester by bus at six in
the morning.

This is classical Wrong Approach. To be out of the
ruck be gay. Come into the Egyptian Room, if necessary, with a smile and a wink. Roar with laughter as
you approach the neolithic flints. If with a young
child, it is possible to increase this effect and sustain
your reputation for child management at the same
time by occasionally feeding it with the special glu-
cose sweets we supply—dashed with opium or some
other not quite harmless somniferent. "I think it's
because we never say 'Don't'," you say to a group of
friends who are admiring the child's acquiescence.
"She is rather sweet, isn't she?"

Practise on the Tate.

It is as well to practise all gambits on the permanent museums and exhibits before approaching any special collections or centenary shows.

Practise in the Tate Gallery, for instance, not to shuffle grimly from picture to picture, not to hang one methodical minute before each exhibit. To achieve the one-up position, let it be known that you have "come to see the Steers." This refers of course to Steer the artist. Say that there is one particular Steer of aluminous seascape with a patch of elephant grey (do not say "a small battleship") on the horizon and if it is not on view it must be in the vaults and can you please have access to them.

It is a fairly good gambit, certainly at the Tate, to be friendly with the attendants. At any rate address them by some name such as "Kemp," and say, "Good morning, Kemp. Is Mr. Laver in to-day?" "Mr. Laver" is what is called an "O.K. exhibition name." Or you can say, "Good afternoon, McIndoe, have you seen Sir Kenneth?"

With pictures, and with art in general, it is rather a good thing not to go to the places where everybody else goes. E.g., avoid the air-conditioned room at the National Gallery unless you can say that you personally had a hand in mixing the air or advised on the mean warmed-upness. Change the subject and talk instead about something almost completely inaccessible.

"Have you ever seen that little collection at the Walthamstow Waterworks?" you can ask. "Chiefly Saxon, of course, Saxon coins picked out of the King's Scholars' Pond Sewer. The design is debased Roman, and if you are as absurdly keen on debased Roman as I am, you won't grudge an hour or two at Walthamstow."

Be fairly ruthless, I think, with opponents of "modern" painting. If you are lucky enough to find a man who still says, "I don't know about pictures, but I know what I like," point out to him that because he does not know about pictures he does not know what he likes, and repeat this in a thundering voice. If he whimpers back something about it all being too advanced for him, point out exactly how many years Cezanne died before he was born, and the precise date of the exhibition of the first Modiglianis in London. Exaggerate both these dates and say, "after all, Matisse and your great-grandmother are exact contemporaries." If your man says of some picture, "Yes, but what does it mean?" ask him, and keep on asking him, what his carpet means, or the circular patterns on his rubber shoe-soles. Make him lift up his foot to look at them.

The safest subject for criticism is the accuracy of the descriptive notice. At Kew Gardens it is no bad thing, when wandering through the shades of the collection of elm-tree species, to read out "Ulmus flavescens" from the label and say, "It's not, now, classified as a true elm at all." Or with a display of musical instruments, better still, read out, "Violin by Armedio, 1760–1820," and then say, "1760, of course, is complete and utter guesswork."

It is always possible, when in doubt, to criticize "the lack of information for ordinary simple people like myself."

Another useful ploy is to criticize something for what it isn't, even if what it isn't isn't what it is trying to be.

For example, take an exhibition of beautiful books. The basic gambit (since the object of the Exhibition is to demonstrate the aesthetic quality of the type, binding, &c.) is to say *plonkingly* that "to me personally a book is something to be read."

You can then pick up three books at random and say of No. 1 that "you'd like to read it if you could see the wood for the trees"; of No. 2 that "the binding is certainly expensive, but does the book fall open *easily and naturally?*" and of No. 3 (*Paradise Lost*, printed in italics) you can say, "Of course if you like reading poetry at an angle . . . but after ten pages I should be in italics myself." You can raise a laugh by leaning sideways when saying this.[2]

In the same way, at the pottery part of an exhibition it is always possible to say, "What a pity there is no example of Leeds Glaze."

When looking at plants or animals in any kind of Natural History show or zoo or gardens just say, "Oh, but it is not the same . . . not the same behind bars." You can say that all round the rock garden at Kew, for instance.

"Pyrenean Iris. Oh yes, yes, yes, but terrible. Terrible if one has ever been overcome by the miracle of this thing bravely clasping the crevice of the perpendicular cliff-face at Luchesse—terrible to see it here, tamed and humbled by man."

I like and recommend this gambit.

Special Exhibition Ploy.

For crowded buildings and special exhibitions remember, in general, that you are different from the crowd. For instance, if the notice says "Turn Left," instantly turn right. Do not trudge round in a crocodile. If there is an injunction to keep moving, stand stock still, eyes fixed on the ceiling.

---

[2] Students must not be confused if, after reading this paragraph, they are left with a feeling that they are not quite certain which side they are meant to be on. If we are continually expected to take sides, that is the end of argument.

Again, to suggest that you have the artistically awakened eye and can form your own opinion in perfect independence of the kind of judgment which the lay-out and emphasis of the exhibition seems to demand, pause a long time before some object which has nothing to do with the exhibits—say a fire extinguisher or a grating in the floor through which warmed-up museum air rises—and say, "The influence of William Morris, even here," or just, "Now *that*, to me, is a beautiful object."

The best way to praise the exhibition is to say, "It's a great jaunt, a delightful affair, and a huge success. Exhibitions always are a huge success."

You can then criticize.

After showing that you yourself are a jolly and exhibition-minded person, and have enjoyed, in the old days at the White City, the model of the Astronomer Royal in margarine, you can then be generally nasty by complaining that this particular show lacks the indefinable something, the gaiety, perhaps, of the Petit Palais Exhibition at Varence in 1931 (designed by Pompipier), or the feeling for Internationalism which one got frightfully from that wonderful Fülden-bliegen Collection in the Rond Tor at Uppsala. Behaviouristically, one should be alert and clever, also an expert in exhibition technique. Know, especially if in the company of a varicose aunt, how to park your car three miles away and walk, because it saves time in the end. Know how to come in ten minutes before closing time, because that is the only way to see the rooms, in comfort, if rather quickly. Know how to avoid exhibition malaise, how to diet for exhibitions, the importance of light salads with a touch of garlic, because the rooms will smell of garlic anyhow. Know how to keep your mind off what you are looking at,

MUSEUMSHIP: CLEARING THE CROWD
The "All the World Makes Way for Lovers" ploy.

and how to bring pass-the-time puzzles of the kind, for instance, where you separate two twisted nails.

Finally, remember that the best and most overwhelmingly one-up way to go to an exhibition with a person is to be in love with the person and for the person to be in love with you. It is no bad thing to hold hands with the person even if she is not in love with you, so long as she does not look grumpy. It is said, too, that people will instinctively make way for young, or fairly young, lovers. This also puts the exhibition to its right use, as a wooing ground. Experience will suggest how the permanent Exhibitions of London may be utilized. Use as guide Billington's OLD WICKET GATE list (Billington's Woo Aids) of Museum Meeting Grounds.

List entries include a brief description of the kind of girl whom it is suitable to arrange to meet in Room 6 (English Glass) at the V and A, or the quite different girl you meet by the Beaverbrook at the Tate. And the third type, equally distinct in *climate of attraction,* is the girl you will meet under the Epstein frieze at the St. James's Park Tube Station.

Don't forget also that there is a fourth type of girl whom you will meet by the East entrance of the Zoological Gardens. You must use your own judgment whether to refer, jokingly, to the fact that the cages for the birds of prey adjoin the turnstile.

VI

A Note on Litmanship

In a popular American biography of the Founder the following statement occurs: "In tracing the evolution of Gamesmanship, too little stress is placed on Potter's early work 'The Muse in Chains' (? 1937)." For the "Eng. Lit." described in the early chapters of this once forgotten volume, prized item now in book sales, differs little from the Art of Knowing about English Literature without Actually Reading Any Books—our own working definition of Litmanship as taught at Yeovil.

EVERY YEAR hundreds nay thousands of young lads and lasses pass through the English Literature courses in the Universities of this Island. How to help them?

Many students come to us when it is too late, their

brains permanently damaged by the dread litticosis. "But I have worked it, worked it out," I once heard a lass of twenty continually repeating. "If I read all the books I am supposed to read I shall be 187 years old before I . . . 187 . . . " The rest of the sentence was broken.[1]

Yet ten days later this lass was alert and happy, and was leaving our walls, a qualified Lifegirl, to face her Finals Year with new courage. I had noticed how different she looked after attending the first lecture by our Gorboduc Reader, on "First-Hand Knowledge My Foot."

Before she left I asked her, as she handed over her modest fee, what had particularly helped her.

"Textmanship," she answered, with a shy smile.

Let us give you this one glimpse, then, of what had helped Josephine. Textmanship. How, that is, not only to write an essay about,[2] but *to give detailed comments on the wording* of an examination set book

[1] "And what about Bandello?" I actually replied, with a grim smile, because we must suppose she was supposed to read the Italian Sources and the Sources of the Sources too.

[2] Old Yeovillers will understand that in her first lecture Josephine will have been told how to deal with some classic novel—*Wuthering Heights* is taken as type of book student will have heard of but not read—and write about it (a) as if she had read all other possible novels of the same type ("Middle Period of the Novel of Passion") or (b) as if Brontë was a bit of a copy cat ("she shows, in her rapid transition from the vast to the intimate, the influence, first, of the literary heirs of *Werther*, second, of the Burney school of domestic observations.")

without having actually read it. This is known as Gobbetship.

Gobbetship.

The gobbet, hitherto the bugbear of all examinations in English Literature, is a selection of quotations from a Set Book or Set Text. First we harden students, immunise them, against the intimidating wording of such examination questions. (*"State exactly what you know of the following. Do NOT answer more than SEVEN of the ASTERISKS."*)

Then we teach them what to say. Specimen author, typically, Shakespeare. Specimen play (utterly typically), *Henry IV, Part Two*. Specimen orders: "Annotate the following." Specimen quotation for annotation might be "The slings and arrows of outrageous fortune" except that this is (a) miles too easy, and (b) from *Hamlet*. More likely a line like this, purposely chosen to put you off:

Who keeps the gate here, ho!

Faced with this ridiculous line, what is the examined Lifeboy to do? All that is necessary is to have read a précis of the plot. Then make use of:

1. *The character ploy,* and write:

One of Shakespeare's subtle touches. Note how even the request for a gate to be opened can reveal the impetuousness of the bluff speaker, the lordly peremptoriness of one accustomed to be obeyed.

Without even knowing the *name* of the speaker, it is possible to go on and on about character, e.g.:

This play, full of warriors and their retainers, kings and lords, might be termed a study in the terminology of feudal modes of address.

(Students are recommended to learn above phrase by heart.)

2. *The compression ploy.*

Quote from the Intro. to your school edition, starting "This line":

This line is typical of Shakespeare's middle-to-late historical period in its compression (essence of poetry). Earlier, Shakespeare could well have written "What ho!" instead of "ho!"

3. *Imagery Ploy.*

Note how Shakespeare employs metaphors suitable to the soldier or the man "in use of war's account." [3] "Keeps the gate—Keeps the watch" is the imagery of the military man.

4. *Ti-TUM Ti-TUM Ploy.*

If you know that a regular blank verse line is made up of five Ti-TUMS you can look for irregularities such as—here—the start with TUM-ti and say:

[3] One can soon get the knack of making up Shakespearish quotations like above.

Note the reversed stress of the first foot, a rhythmic variation which Shakespeare allowed himself more and more frequently once he freed himself from the bonds of metre.

It is possible to intensify the effect of this rather thin comment by (a) being scholarly and referring to 18 per cent of TUM-ti (say "trochaic") openings and (b) by shooting off some O.K. prose. Thus:

With what gaiety Shakespeare shook off the chains of metre, drawing the fine Toledo blade of his poetic mastery from the rusty scabbard of rules.[4]

It is rather a good thing, in general, to be keen on Shakespeare's freedom from fetters, and when saying that he was not a thin-lipped scholar poring over books, to use:

5. *The Essentially Theatre Ploy,* and say how bald and inexpressive the line looks *read,* "but speak it and the whole thing leaps to life. Sometimes we forget that *Henry IV,* Part Two, was a play, and to be acted."

Less recommended and now definitely less O.K., and in fact shelved for a few years is:

6. *The Voice of Shakespeare Ploy.* A pity, because it was always possible to say up to 1925 that any two consecutive words "show Shakespeare's personal evolutions at this period." Why, at this time, for instance, "the reiterated suggestion of closed doors and castles, prisons and castellations? Is it not that impending

_____
[4] Learn this by heart, too.

75

sense of claustrophobic doom and frustration which preceded Shakespeare's tragic period?"

7. *"Shakespeare's Theatre" Ploy.* If by any miracle Lifeboy happens to know that this quotation is the first line of the play, or even if not, he can nowadays do much better than (6) by referring to early inn-yard theatres, upper and lower stages, and the use made of them in such a line as this.

Finally 8. *Punctuation Ploy.*

Point out that there is no proof that the punctuation is Shakespeare's and if it was (?) instead of (!) or especially (! !) at the end of the line, the whole sense would be changed. This is good gambiting. Super-gambiting is to show you are:

9. *Versed in The language of Shakespeare and his Contemporaries,* and go on like this:

Who . . . here, ho! "Who" is here, I think, the in-definite (= "He who"), and not the interrogative pro-noun, as is implied, for instance, by the punctuation, "Who keeps the gate here? ho!" (*Oxford Shakespeare*), and "Who keeps the gate here, ho?" (*Cambridge Shake-speare*). "Who keeps the gate" is a periphrases (= "Por-ter") of a kind usual in calling to servants or others, in attendance but out of sight. Cf. *Henry VIII.* V.ii.2, 3: "*Cran* . . . Ho! Who waits there!" Cf. also Beaumont and Fletcher, *Maid's Tragedy,* V.iii: "*Lys* . . . Summon him, Lord Cleon. *Cleon:* Ho, from the walls there!"; and *Jack Straw* (Hazlitt's *Dodsley,* V.396): "Neighbours, you that keep the gates."

This last gambit, shortened by two thirds from Lifemanship's Arden Edition of Shakespeare, needs training even if every single reference is made up. It is not known whether the above are.

L.C.C. Postgraduate

SOME SIMPLE USES OF LITMANSHIP

Are You Fond of Reading?

I LIKE TO finish these sections with examples of our applied instruction for postgraduates.

What is the use, Litmen are often asked, of being able to read Chaucer's *Prologue* in the original if you don't know what to do with it in after-life? It is precisely in such a Lifesituation as this that we like to feel we can be of most use.

Well-readship.

In a word, how to appear well read. How to appear, without giving books more than a casual glance, for surely there is not time, that no man is quicker than yourself off the mark with the latest thriller, newest white paper on the development of opencast tungsten mining, or most recent Reminiscences of some un-heard-of nephew of Dante Gabriel Rossetti.

Coad-Sanderson was always my model here, and it was I who created him our Longfellow Reader at

A CORNER OF THE LIBRARY

Note here the new student (**H**), breaking fingernails on dummy books. *How will he deal with this situation?* Note desk with signatures of former students. Note empty bust-case. *One day it might be You.* On left, genuine books. (**D**) *Gamesmanship* and *Lifemanship.* (**F**) The complete works of all 19th-century novelists in six volumes (shortened). (**G**) Classic French literature (abbreviated and epitomised for easy reading).

L.C.C. He ate, drank, and slept the new books. Wallpaper controller, with income of £720 p.a., and a mother and step-mother to support, as well as his step-mother's step-children, Coad could afford to buy very few books indeed. His methods were and are: (1) To collect book jackets from a dear old reviewer, Horton, whom he knows and who helps him. These jackets he wraps round old books so that his library seems to be in a constantly refreshed and up-to-date state. He has also (2) beautifully developed the technique of Upright Reading—that is to say, perusing books in bookshops without actually buying them.[5] He also (3) reads the kind of reviews which enable you to criticise a book without having actually read

---

[5] The fact that Coad hardly read the books he possessed or that these were few in number was never revealed. Coad was himself deeply influenced by the brilliant specialisations of (Miss) S. Arnold-Forster on Marginaliaship and the ! Ploy. Miss Arnold-Forster has perfected a means of suggesting to borrowers of books that their reading is superficial and that they are imperceptive of the finer nuances. This is done by underlinings, comments, &c. written onto the margins of the book at random *in ink*.

"Surely" ploy:

> At this time William Cowper had at last settled down with six cats in the Middle Temple.

Surely by 1753

Question-mark ploy:

> It might be said that Sarah Coleridge's childhood in the Lakes may have profoundly influenced her poetic development.

?

Exclamation-mark ploy:

> Maria Edgeworth's early experiences in the Liverpool slums brought home to her that drink is indeed an evil mocker, and she remained a total abstainer all her life.

!!!

it, and finally (4) he keeps certain blocks of type-written manuscripts always on show and will some-times say "Willie Maugham allowed me to browse through this before he made the final corrections. There was little I could say which was of any value to him, I fear."

It might be supposed that Coad-Sanderson, in order to maintain his gambit, would have to read fifteen books a week.

He was saved from this stupefying task by two strong subqualifications, as we call them. The first: Coad was an Old Reviewer himself. He knew that there are only five things which can under any con-ceivable circumstance be said for, not more than eight to be said against, any known book.[6]

It is also possible, within the five minutes, to learn five words to quote (supposed to be a certain way of proving that you have read the book through). Re-member that any five consecutive words taken out of *any dramatic* passage of a novel or *deeply passionate* section of a poem will sound both forced and absurd if repeated by you on the top of a tram, while mixing a drink, or while the person you are speaking to is filling up a form.

If by chance you yourself happen to have read a

[6] Not only O.K. Literary Names, with Rilking (see *Lifemanship*, p. 65) are taught at L.C.C., but basic O.K. critical phrases (with intonations) as well. No matter if they tell us very little of the ob-ject to be criticised; their main function is to tell everybody ("I'm

book on the morning of publication, Coad could always go one better. I have myself rushed round to Coad with a copy of, say, T. D. Pontefract's *The Tea Party* at eleven o'clock—two hours after it was issued— to see if I could for once be one up on him over a new book. I do not remember what he said, but experience has taught me it must have been either (*a*) "Let me lend you the American edition. It's beautifully printed and it hasn't got that stupid cut on page 163." Or (*b*) (*more simply*) "Good old Pontefract— still churning them out."

Rather Delightfulship") what an extraordinarily nice chap you, the critic, are. E.g., *O.K. critical lines:*

(1) "Thank goodness there's no mention of Freud"

OR

"Personally I'm sick of the Oedipus complex" (there need not of course be any reference to Freud or complexes in the work concerned).

(2) "Delightfully fresh and spontaneous."

Both (1) and (2) will suggest that the critic, in spite of his rather scruffy appearance, *is himself pretty fresh and spontaneous.*

(3) "A rewarding experience."

("Rewarding" is the new O.K. word for 1952. "Climate of thought" has eighteen weeks to run.)

O.K. Attacks:

(4) "Personally I found the love-scenes rather embarrassing."

(5) "There is a certain archness which I found displeasing."

(4) and (5) mean *"Though sensitive and cultured my peasant stock ensures that I am O.K. for passion."*

(6) Quote misquotations of commas.

(7) Complainingly quote clichés, or at any rate say, "Why must 'blood' always be 'congealed'," as if it *was* a cliché.

(8) In criticising any translation, take any five lines of the translation and then quote the original and say "Why not let's have the original, so much more force and point &c." If the original language is Syriac, so much the less chance of argument.

This answer (*b*) brings me to the second subquali-
fication which made things more possible for Coad in
his pursuit of Keeping Abreastmanship. There are
latest books and latest books, he would imply; and
after he reached the age of forty-four, when reading
became even more difficult for him, he would make a
tremendous point, though as up to date as ever, of
only buying the books "which interested him."

"Look, I've got a prize," he would say to me. "I've
got it too," said I breathlessly, pointing to my new
Simon Halliday.

"Ah, good, good," Coad says now. "But I didn't
actually mean that one. Where does the Mysterious
Religious Character come in this time? Chapter
XIV?"

This maddened me, (*a*) because I had in fact been
rather moved by Chapter XIV, and (*b*) because I
knew Coad was going to pull out some small almost
privately printed book and say, "I meant this— John's
new book on the architecture of lift shafts. It's almost
frightfully good."

I have said sufficient, I think, to show Coad's
gambit. And what, you will say, of the counter? For
each ploy has its anti. Coad is counter-proof, but there
is a way of making the average new-bookman feeble.
It is based on a remark made 125 years ago next
March by that domineering Lifeman, Charles Lamb.

Lamb said, when any of his friends bought a new

book, he bought an old one. This, in my view, is difficult to beat, as a ploy. There is an answer to it. Play
can be made with the period flavour of ivory-tower-
ship, as a gambit. Yet on the whole it is quite a fair
ploy, and the only reason we sometimes frown on it
is that, containing as it does a grain of truth, the
taste remaining in the mouth is scarcely a pleasant
one.

"WHO KEEPS THE GATE HERE, HO!"

It was only when we began to act the line on our actual stage that
we realised that the words should be spoken outside the door, not
inside, as, wrongly, here.

PART TWO

THE "HOUSE PARTY"

Origin of the "House Party"

The title "Lifemaster"—what does it mean, what does it stand for?

In the old days it stood for a thorough course at the Lifemanship College, including such extras as Foreign Languaging and Manglo-Relations. These were not optional. The test was severe. Credits were necessary in 18 of the 22 subjects, and the candidates must have satisfied the examiners in at least one subject of London Matriculation.

But there were many promising students who found this insistence on mere scholastic ability a permanent bar to high office. A profession where personality was so important needed a new test. It was for this purpose that the House Party was created. It is an institution copied now, I am glad to report, very honorably, we need not say by whom.*

In essence our House Party is a friendly enough affair, in which young Lifemen visit us as guests (for list of fees see back page of pamphlet) and are made to feel uneasy, of course, but not aggressively so, while they on their part make their student attempts to undermine our natural one-upness.

We watch our candidates, of course, without their knowing it, although they are all aware of this being watched without knowing it. As they drive the car or wield rod or gun, field glass or wine glass, qualities of Lifeleadership and the reverse are quickly spotted. Few may there be to fail to be awarded the title, with its additional fee, of Lifemaster.

---

* No harm in saying in a footnote. It has been adopted by The Foreign Office Selection Board.

87

"RECEIVING DAY"

A group of us ready to welcome the new batch of week-end "guests." On the left, Odoreida, with Cogg-Willoughby in characteristic pose. On the right, Ivy Spring and Gattling-Fenn.

VII

The Carmanship of Godfrey Plaste

SOMETIMES the Lifemaster Candidate at the House Party is under inspection before he realises it.

Take, for instance, the journey down, by train or car. Perhaps he will have some lifetutor as companion. If in a car, he is supposed to know something of car theory, and to have read our pamphlet, here reproduced in shortened form, on *Carmanship: or the art of stealing the crown of the road without being an absolute hog.*

Godfrey Plaste, our Buick Reader in Carmanship and for many years referee at the Gameslife Students' Sportsground, Yeovil, must have written nearly a third of a million words on the various Lifemanship gambits associated with his almost too passionate spare-time interest in car and driver play. Never **satis-fied**, Plaste tore up sheet after sheet as he wrote, sometimes even before, until at last only four complete pages remained. These he handed over, with a rather fulsome dedication, to myself, expressing a hope that I would not publish.

As this "wish" was obviously only a gambit, now that Plaste has passed on I am giving what I hope is the gist of Plaste's pages here, trying as it were to reconstruct from the fourth lumbar vertebra the skeleton of a Plastiploy.

As is admitted, Godfrey's motor play came from one primary gambit which he evolved over many years. It is known—easy phrase to remember—as "Plaste's Placid Salutation," and I am bound to say he brought this to a fine art.

A ferociously selfish driver, Plaste gloried in bringing approaching limousines to a dead stop by choosing the wrong moment to overtake. I have myself seen an oncoming quadruple tank carrier forced by Plaste's carefully timed passing to mount the verge and melt through a concrete lamp-standard. Yet Plaste got away with it by this "salutation." In essence this was a simple raising of the hand, an inclination of the head, and a grave smile. Instead of the scream of rage one would expect from the oncomers, they would often *actually salute back*.

PLASTE'S PLACID SALUTATION

Why was this? The only time I met Plaste on the road head-on he was passing an ambulance. Noticing the ambulance bell, I had slowed down and pulled well over. It was one of the narrowest two-lane traffic sections of the notorious Great North Road. Suddenly the light blue nose of Plaste's battered little sedan, screaming in some low gear, crept out behind. I almost drove the brakes through the floor. As my head hit the windscreen, I saw the hand raised slowly in salute.

There was something so calm and dignified about this gesture that I can only say that instead of anger I was made to feel that I had somehow helped; that some message of urgency for the nation had passed that way, a second saved, a crisis averted. I am not sure that I didn't salute back. It was only afterwards, looking back and recognizing the honeycomb of dents on the mudguards of Plaste's wretched car, that I became angry, and slowly began to shout.

91

It was the success of this gambit of his which set Plaste thinking in terms of carmanship.

Ever since he was a child he has been fascinated by Back-seat Drivership (the Beastly Passenger ploy), a palaeo-gambit which existed before Gamesmanship and Yeovil were thought of. Plaste's passenger technique was first to remain absolutely silent for five or six minutes.

Long before it was necessary for me to brake he would fidget with his feet, but slightly. Then, when it

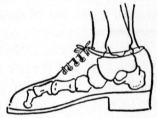

PLASTE AS PASSENGER (From an X-ray photograph.)

We were fortunate to obtain this record of the position of Plaste's left foot, made at the moment when, using the Lifeman's "art which reveals art" (Morteroy) he "instinctively" brakes as his driver approaches a roundabout. Note particularly the flexure—almost a flexion—of Distal and Middle Phalanges, to suggest that driver's speed is carelessly excessive.

was known that I should have to left turn, he would stretch his left arm far out of the car, half a mile before the turning point, and for a right turn lift his extended hand up and down as if he were scrambling eggs, thus making a dangerous Highway Code error and suggesting that my hand signals were in-effective at the same time.

If we approached a child under the age of twelve walking quietly along the footpath, he would first wince, then draw up his knees, then say, "Toot toot" quietly under his breath.

PLASTE: Toot-toot.
SELF: What did you say?
PLASTE: Only "toot-toot" . . . I wasn't quite sure whether you'd seen that child on the footpath.
SELF (*pause*): But it's walking into the house.
PLASTE: Oh, yes. All right now. Exquisite little thing.

But if the tables were turned and he was driving, Plaste had amazing powers of making his passengers feel beastly. If, after driving at full speed across three dangerous crossings, he was about to emerge, as he once was, I remember, from Wallingford onto the main Oxford Road in Henley Week, I did say, smil-ing, "By the way, major road ahead." Plaste stopped his car instantly, and drew it into the side.

"Look," he said. "Do you mind if I tell you some-thing? I have been driving a car for twenty-five years and if any passenger is going to tell me what to do he brings to the realm of the conscious the very thing which experience has happily made intuitive and natural. I do not mind bad manners, but I do mind death. Thank you." Of course what he said was absolutely right, and as he dashed out into the Oxford Road and tipped off his front wing against a beer lorry, I began to mumble apologies.

"Forget it," he said to me.

Plaste had another method of "softening" his passengers. He had in his locker a collection of out-of-date and crumpled maps made at very different dates to very different scales, and through long wear rubbed into illegibility round the creases. He would hand a bunch of these to me and say, "How about a little map reading?" After ten minutes finding the right map and another ten finding the right place Plaste would say, "I say, do you mind keeping that map in the right folds?"

"Yes," I said—really slightly pulling his leg. Then after another two minutes:

"Well?" he would say.

"What do you mean, 'Well?'?" I would say.

"Where are we?"

"Getting on," I said. (We were now half-way between Nettlebed and Henley.)

Plaste began to use his quiet voice: "Yes, yes, but I mean where are we? I mean, it makes it so much more interesting."

"We're not anywhere exactly."

"What do you—I wonder what that rather jolly little wood over there is called?"

After about three minutes' twisting and turning of the map I reply, "It says 'Upper Common'."

Plaste would then irritate me by using the annoying word "Folkmoot" and saying, "Doesn't that touch your imagination? Perhaps in this Common Land the Folkmoot was once held; the clearing in the forest."

With women map readers Plaste was even quieter and more incisive. He would say very clearly and slowly, "All set, my dear? Now look, we want the second third-class road to the left."

"To the left on the map?" most women would reply.

"How do you mean?" Plaste would say, rather charmingly. Then: "Are you orientated?"

After a pause the woman might say, "Won't there be a signpost?" To this Plaste replied, "What?" Still smiling he would make elaborate hand signals and draw in to the side. "I expect we've overshot it, haven't we? Let's see if I can find the place."

After four or five minutes of this, few women could tell the difference between a railway line and a reservoir, and there would be one of those lapses into tearful silence which satisfied Plaste so much.

This, I hope, will give the student what may be called Plaste definitive. For the rest, it is a scribbled note here, a word-of-mouth tradition there. Godfrey ployed his last ploy three years ago sadly enough, self-gambited. A collision while driving in reverse.

How did this come about? One of Plaste's most feverishly irritating techniques, we are told, was his knowledge-of-Londonship. He would go a whole mile off route to wind his way through some good yard because it was the "only way of avoiding the Notting Hill traffic." To complain that this would not affect your journey to Swiss Cottage anyhow would be to play into Plaste's hands. He would "know some parking place" under a disused railway bridge only accessible by taxi. He would know "definite spots in parks where there could be no speed trap" and use his information by speeding at 50 m.p.h. round and round the Victoria Monument outside Buckingham Palace, for instance—quite useless of course. Finally, and fatally, Plaste would always approach one-way streets from the wrong end and then go up them backwards. "Saves time," he said.[1] It was while performing this evolution that he reversed at 30 m.p.h. into a car which was approaching in the correct direction at a similar speed.

Too late, alas, for Plaste to leap out of his car, his usual practice when he hit somebody, and cry, "Did you get that man's number?" We have the Plaste car

[1] Having spent nine months' practice in backing, this one branch of his driving was good, and as a wooman Plaste managed to keep one girl faithful to him for two and a half years by constantly demonstrating his virtuosity in reverse.

in our Yeovil museum, though it is not usually on show. Not of any make, it was originally put together from spare parts by C. Plaste, G. Plaste's nephew, son of V. Plaste, the iron railing manufacturer. The bonnet looked feebler than nine horse, but beneath it was, in fact, an old 17-h.p. engine with six cylinders, noisy enough, but impressive when "G.P." slipped into third and said, "Not bad for nine horses."

The engine pinked like a chime of bells. "Must do," said Plaste proudly, "with this little tiger, built for hotted-up aviation spirit." In the back of the car is the string of tin medals out of crackers which Plaste referred to as "Médailles d'Honneur Club Belgique." There on the back seat are the tyre chains "with special spikes for the Courboise Pass . . . Monte Carlo Rally." [2] On the dash of his car, examine the starter button which is a dummy. Plaste would press this useless button, and then say, "Never mind, half a jiff."

I can see him now, whisking out three adjustable spanners, and then his long pink bony wrists would disappear under the bonnet where the normal starter

[2] I have been asked in the preparation of this book to insert a footnote on the Monte Carlo Rally, or Rallyship,* as I prefer to call it. As I myself go in for a different type of dangerous driving, I am in process, through conversations, of stabilising the rules of Rallyship with Carlo One (R. Walkerley) who is in close touch with

* This footnote is highly technical, and should be read only by those who have achieved some record time round some record track. We ourselves hold a record for Silverpebble, having lapped it at 14 m.p.h. in an unblown Bean.

button was concealed. "Got it," he would say, as the engine miraculously leapt into action, while the female passenger exclaimed with admiration at what

---

many fellow drivers at the Carburettor Club, which maintains its delightful atmosphere of incomprehensibly technical gambiting. Thus (at random):

A: Last Saturday! . . .

B: What?

A: You were fairly streaking along at Bedtimber.

B: Oh, I don't know. We dropped 900 revs on the second lap—just as you passed me.

A: Did I pass you—no, you were Number Ten, weren't you? I'd got my eyes so glued on the tail of Farina . . .

Rallyman A wins, with his suggestion that he was only really concerned with super-ace rivals.

The Carburettor Club has its own set of ploys belonging to what they term the Dicing with Death group or Dicemanship. Here are the two basic approaches, nicknamed the Walkerley Talkerleys.

DICEMAN A: Actually I was petrified. No anchors whatever, after two laps, so I suppose I did go rather fast round those corners. Actually, I was a bit shaken.

DICEMAN B: I know. But for some unearthly reason it seems to go the other way with me. You know that little Silverpebble incident when I lost a wheel? I went sort of calm and rather cold. I seemed to have bags of time to pull up on the grass, get out, and walk away. But, lord, was I scared, later, when I thought about it.

Here is a parlette of Drink-diceman, interesting if only because it gives a perfect example of the riposte or anticounter:

A: Drink?

B: No thanks. Got to drive on Saturday.

A: Well, speaking absolutely personally, I'm scared to get into the car unless I'm practically completely stinkaroo. (*He roars with laughter.*)

This is good ploying as everybody thinks that A, who has built up an atmosphere of never drinking anything but Coca-Cola, is amusing and decent. Everybody that is but B, who knows that A always uses a private flask before a race.

98

appeared to be a miracle of mechanical comprehension, deftness, and male mastery. There is no Plaste Memorial, but the simple, common nettles along the west side of our sports ground have remained uncut. He would have wished it so.

VIII

The Carter-Williams
Railway Gambits

"I KNOW Carter-Williams personally," said a young House Party guest to me one Friday, hoping to impress as he stepped out not of a car but the third-class compartment of a railway carriage, holding a first-class ticket in his hand. I approved of his sound railway-ticket play, with its suggestion of affluence devoid of snobbery; but I had to pull him up on "Carter-Williams."

"Which do you mean?" I said, for of course B. Carter and J. Williams, though known to each other, are two totally distinct persons, young National Service men who as sergeants were expert in furloughship, as we used to call it, and studied railwayship over a prolonged period of leave-fiddling. Far apart

in conveyed climate as each terminus is, the Eustonian and Paddingtonian approach are basically similar, at the deepest level.[1]

There is of course one essential railway gambit in which each student is supposed to perfect himself. But

THE BASIC RAILWAYSHIP OF COGG

Note: the book is Ruskin's *Unto This Last*. The names of other books can be supplied.

before reminding you of this, which always comes at the close of our railway pamphlet, a reminder of Cogg-Willoughby and his railway work.

[1] "The Underground is the Great Leveller" was first said by the amazing John Stuart Mill *at the age of four,* only two and one half years after he first mastered the Greek alphabet. Some part of our Fifth Volume, 1956, will be devoted to precocityship and its counter, Miltoning, sometimes defined as the art of not writing *Paradise Lost* before fifty.

Cogg has only one railway gambit, and it is simple. It is to use the railway.

"I never go by car," he says. "Goodness no."

So even, say, between Redhill and Dorking, he will take the frightfully old-fashioned electrified rail system. Portsmouth to London by rail is typical Cogg. And his total effect, of course, is to be alone, to be clean, especially about the fingernails, to be unruffled, to read, and to go first-class with a third-class ticket—the reverse of the procedure we normally recommend. He also uses a cigarette-holder—quite unlike his normal character this—but effective, I am bound to say, with his thin discriminating temples and the vulnerable effect of his prematurely bald head. He wears horn-rimmed glasses designed by Chermayeff and *gloves while reading.*

He is usually sitting alone, occasionally nonsmoking in a smoker, nice touch. And always quite clean, and calm. All this is aimed, need we say, at the Gattling-Fenns of this world.

Gattling, door to door, can get there seven minutes faster, over the two and a quarter hour journey, by plunging through wind and traffic in his white and green roadster. But whereas Gattling on arrival is nervy, dishevelled, and half his normal size with the desire for a drink, Cogg-Willoughby steps out of his taxi ironed and tidied, and poisedly asks for soda-water.

But to return to Carter-Williams. As young militia-
men they made great game, on long-distance journeys
with dining cars, of pretending to have dinner on
both the first and second service while really eating
sandwiches or even nothing, and vice versa—a lot of
horseplay, to my mind.

But they did pick up a surprising amount of rail-
ship lore, and made a few converts with their slap-
dash slogan—BE TOP MAN—WIN THE JOUR-
NEY.

Little Wootton Ploy.

Superior knowledge of the route was one method.[2]
("Little Wootton Play" is the random naming of in-
decipherable stations after they have flashed by.) In
the dark at speed I have myself found it possible to
convince passengers that I know the position of the
train *by sounds*. I say:

SELF: "That loop of the Ouse is on our right now."
     (No need to say which of the fourteen Ouses you
     are referring to.)

[2] To describe method two I will quote direct from Carter:
  On the first reference by any of his travelling companions to
the heat or stuffiness of the compartment, J. Williams would leap
to his feet, open all the windows and the door into the corridor,
and *turn the heating off*. He would then put on coat, gloves,
and muffler, and wait.
  The counter-ploy to this, of course, is to take off your jacket,
loosen your collar, and *appear to enjoy* the fresh air. But this
move has never been used since *Healthman's Disaster*, when two
determined Lifemen, travelling on the Flying Scotsman, arrived
in Edinburgh frozen, almost incredibly, to death.

PASSENGER: "How on earth do you know?"
SELF: "That rattle of points and then the rap as we
went under the footbridge. Cobb's Corner."

Actually this patter was used against me by the
dignified driver of the Coronation Scot. It was only
afterwards that I discovered there was no footbridge
and no Ouse.

At the end of their pamphlet, Carter-Williams describe Rail Primary—the gambit we all practise yet
never perfect. And how often in fact we fail in—
what? In *Terminus Technique.*

There are still men, albeit the layest of the lay,
who, coming into Euston, will begin fidgeting even
before Watford, say, "Are we here," begin to button
some sort of dingy mackintosh, take down suitcase,
and remain standing, meaninglessly. "New boy," we
all intone at him in a repeated plainsong—but are we
always perfect ourselves?

Let me quote Carter:

If you are truly established as Top Man, your fellow
passengers will leave you to judge the correct moment.

There are two methods.

1. *The Eustonian.* If the line is well known to you, as
terminus approaches sit absorbed in a book, and make
no preparations for disembarkation until *the very last
minute.* Long practice in our Yeovil dummy railway
carriage makes it possible to snap book shut and get out
smoothly precisely as train stops.

2. *The Paddingtonian.* If you do not know line well enough to employ (1), act as follows. Prepare to leave the train *at least half an hour* before you are likely to reach your destination. Then leave compartment with word about "getting opposite taxi." Lay passengers are left feeling gloomy, apprehensive, and feeble.

IX

Game Birdsmanship

DURING THE FIRST DAY of our Yeovil week-end we encourage candidates to get out and about, either playing games according to methods recommended by us or taking part in sports often called the "shipless" sports because hitherto nothing has been printed by us on these themes.[1]

But now the time has come to get down on paper some basic code for shooting, fishing, &c, encouraging our Yeovil demonstrators [2] in each subject to say something of their technique.

[1] Nothing printed but plenty talked. For three years, shooting men of all denominations, yes and fishermen too, have been sending in messages, "advise" here, "pronounce" there. "Coarse Fishermen Expect a Lead from Yeovil" is a headline some may have seen in the journalism of this sport.

[2] These sporting life demonstrators are not on the regular Yeovil staff nor are they permanent. The office is held for one year during

Gifted Colonel F. Wilson, illustrator of our manuals, and often quite welcome when an extra beater is wanted, is Gunpowder Reader in Game Birdsmanship and avers that the whole craft needs a thorough spring cleaning.

We are certainly cutting out, I hope, a good deal of dead wood. The man who trains his dog to go out quick after the drive and pick birds indiscriminately from all the way down the line—this man is no gamesman and should not so name himself.[3] And there is something too like boasting even about Gattling-Fenn's reply to his host's "You must have got over twenty birds there" . . .

"No, only nineteen came."

A good deal of Gamebirding work has been done recently on the subject of luncheon in butt or by hedgerow.

Gattling and Cogg-Willoughby are contrasted here. Cogg goes in for especially luxurious luncheon hampers, better than anybody else's, with special instruments, e.g., for cracking the shells of hard-boiled eggs. Gattling contrastingly produces a tin of ham

which three lectures are given somewhere or other, often in the Off Licence section of a pub. The office is known as Morning Dew Reader, although being able to read is neither an essential nor an invariable requirement. There is no special interest in this.

[3] Away, too, with the man who says, "Care to try my 'Superstrike'? Knock over an elephant at a hundred yards."—and hands his unsuspecting guest a cartridge filled not with normal charge but ordinary toy "caps" for children.

bones with only a few rags of ham left and some dog biscuits. His object (he tells students) is to show how absolutely at one he is with his dog. "He is part of me," says Gattling. Whenever his dog, Fossil, does anything (scratches, takes a left turn, &c) Gattling will say at the same moment something like "Huppah" and add, "You see?" as if what the dog did was the result of his saying "Huppah." After opening the dog biscuits, Gattling sometimes went off with Fossil to drink and even lap water at the same horse-trough.

GATTLING-FENN DEVELOPING DOGMANSHIP TO THE POINT OF ABSURDITY

So much interest was soon aroused by these goings on that people on the fringe of our group would be offering Gattling chicken sandwiches, inexpensive champagne, and so on, so that he always ended by getting a better lunch than anybody.

"How do you do it?" I heard a Mrs. Ems ask Gattling, admiring his dog's obedience.

"Just patience," said Gattling. "Patience. And being rather fond of the creatures."

This annoyed me because I knew that Fossil privately loathed Gattling, and the only objects Fossil could and did pick up effectively were golf balls in play, usually from the first fairway of Huntercombe Golf Course.

One basic we can reveal as emerging in our Yeovil teaching, and that is that clothesmanship for game birdsmen *is perhaps more important than in any other sport.*

I do not wish to publish details of this yet, but would like to draw attention to a gambit of F. Wilson's own, with which we are all particularly wont to associate him personally here, although the "official" name for the gambit is cumbersome ("Wilson's Wali of Swatship"). Its object is to suggest supershot one-upness by reference to first-hand knowledge of jungle sport, if not warfare.

"Nice bit of jungle," is Wilson's opening line. Wilson's next move is to handle his gun in a way which companion finds strange though not yet alarming.

WALIMAN: "Sorry, I'm not used to this."

LAYMAN: "Oh, well."

WALIMAN: "I mean I'm not used to shooting with other people. I used to go out alone. Quite alone.

Except of course for a few natives. It didn't matter if you peppered them."

LAYMAN: "Of course."

WALIMAN: "They liked it because I used to put an anna over each little skin puncture. Sometimes they used to pretend to be knocked out."

WILSON'S BLOODSTAINED ANNA

It was in really cold weather that one saw the perhaps rather hateful side of this Far Eastern play. Wilson would wear a warm-looking sheepskin afghanistan coat or poshteen. From the nice-chap approach Wilson would then offer other poshteens to fellow guns. "Can't do anything with cold fingers."

Wrongly fitted or put on, however, these coats have a trussing-up effect quite fatal, of course, to good shooting. By doing up a certain button, Wilson made wearers feel as if they had been skewered through the armpit. Then Wilson would say: "The Wali of Swat gave me this. I don't know why we sort of hit it off. He laid on a fifteen-gun salute for me. Frightful brigand of course. Here, let me pull this out of your eyes."

GAME BIRDSMANSHIP IN OXON

The Wilson Strait Jacket.

"This" would refer to the Yarkanop hat which Wilson provided as an extra. With its wide loose fur rim it would gradually settle onto the bridge of the nose.

Odoreida was such a bad shot that he could only get himself invited by some stratagem or forgery. Little to report on him, except this variation on the Striking Stranger gambit (see *Lifemanship,* p. 20).

I have always said that Odoreida was repulsive to women; but be that as it may, women were certainly repulsive to him, with the exception of his rather dolphin-breasted sister-in-law Paulette Odoreida, at whom he did once make a somewhat hectoring kind of pass. He did try a little ploying with this quite handsome woman and two young friends, asking if he might bring them too. Once there he would leave these youngish women embarrassingly alone, so that other guns would have to carry them over ditches, or prise apart barbed wire fences with a testy show of chivalry.

GAME BIRDSMANSHIP IN NORFOLK

Mrs. Paulette Odoreida distracting. The colour of her scarf is canary.

Odoreida trained Paulette to wear a gay light yellow scarf and then sit by the butt of a rival. Ocular reflexes caused the birds to turn aside out of range.

GAME BIRDSMANSHIP: BECKETT'S BALK

M. Beckett's suggested technique for grouse shooting. Host sends guests to next line of butts in cars across bumpy track while he rides direct on old and sure-footed pony.

Remember, finally, the importance of the "I'm not just a slayer" approach to this subject, with the man who is interested in the natural history of the thing well in the foreground. But this subject needs a new chapter, and a new guide.

UNSTEADYING EFFECT OF BECKETT'S BALK

Guest (left)   Host (right).

X

Bird Gamesmanship

THE ORIGIN of Bird Gamesing, or Bearded Titman-
ship, is easy to guess. The whole vast ornithoploy
started as a natural history gambit of ordinary game
bird shooting (see last chapter). It was Gilbert White,
when out with his friend D. Barrington, taking pot-
shots at cuckoos, who first said, "Yes, but how does it
rear its young?" after which Barrington never hit a
bird.

Our Zeiss Reader is B. Campbell, who, even if he
was unlucky enough to be sacked from Selborne, still
writes actual bird notes in ornithological papers.
What is the essence of this Birdmanship? he says, in a
large work which will be divided into three volumes.

The first volume will deal with *The Birdsman in
Society* and the two basic ways of making the layman

feel ill at ease. We have adapted these for Yeovil as
follows:

1. In answer to Layman's respectful question to Bird-
man, "Do tell me, is this a good place for birds?" answer,
"Well, no place is bad for birds really, is it?" This is
said in an antiplonking or softly sympathetic voice with
a touch of substitute Richard Jefferies,[1] or at any rate a
"Let me be your Fabre" hint, always annoying.

2. A totally contrasted method can be used for Layman's "Ah, you might be interested about my robin."
Without moving a muscle say, "Certainly, so long as
you're not going to tell me that it (a) taps on your
window or (b) really recognizes you."

This completes the first volume.

"But what do you mean—a whole volume?" newcomers ask.

"Yes."

"But isn't it rather meagre?"

The newcomer is ignorant of the scientific approach. The good birdsman can always fill up by saying whether or not pocket handkerchiefs were worn
by which speaker and if so was it used or if it wasn't,
and other observations especially absolutely unse-
lected, because once you start selecting and therefore
expressing preferences, the scientific attitude and the
whole value of the thing as evidence goes bang. But
Vol. II is certainly more important: *The Birdsman in
the Field.*

---

[1] Hence the term "Jefferieship" for this put-off.

Binocular Play.

Basic Field Birdsman is of course to have the best pair of field glasses in any group. What we teach is the counter to this gambit, the familiarity of which has bred contempt. Method A is to say "There comes a point, I suppose, when if they're too big and cumbrous you can't get them on the bird quickly enough." Counter B is the man who keeps a very small telescope up his trousers leg.

It is worth remembering, we think, that bad old binoculars fit well into bird clothesmanship which

BIRD-CLOTHESMANSHIP BASIC
Classic type (left).

BIRD-CLOTHESMANSHIP BASIC
Modern type, still in experimental stages (right).

surely must consist, basically, as Campbell suggests, in wearing the oldest remains of *two* plus four suits, bound or patched with leather in unusual places, and a hat which before wearing has been left for a week in a chicken run.

Bearded Titmanship.

This is the name given to the art of being in essence one up in the art of spotting uncommon birds.[2] Rivalry in this kind of field work is intense and many a broken nose results, or the words "bigot" or "sewer-rat" are flung back and forth in the correspondence columns of the *Times*. Campbell-recommended par-lettes are as follows:

(a) In the case of a not readily identifiable bird that stays put, birdsman *must* be the first to ask, "Well, what do you think?" which gives him the chance of trapping an unwary diagnosis from his rival. Should this agree with his own private opinion, he jumps in with: "Of course, but the superciliary stripe (or absence of super-ciliary stripe) was a bit unexpected, wasn't it?"

Alternatively,

(b) "I never think it's safe to diagnose at this time of year unless one can see the wing pattern,"

is quite good.

[2] Don't for heaven's sake, say "rare." A bird is rare only if it was "reported over Sheppey in 1908 and one shot by Colonel Westrup in Mull in 1884." No, the rare birds you are looking for, such as the bearded tit, are either "infrequent" or "local."

Tallyship.

This has its own disciples and converts. It consists of keeping *tally* of the number of species observed in one garden, walk, week-end, or hovering over the funnel of the *Bournemouth Queen*. Adepts in this gambit have achieved high virtuosity (recommended method: walk through, e.g., a wood head down and whenever some animal lets out some sort of squeak make mark in notebook and say, e.g., "nut-hatch"). But if tallymen can scarcely be outdone, they can sometimes be made to feel they are doing the wrong thing.

Play the opposite line. Show a sudden liking for watching and continue to watch quite plain and ordinary birds.

"After all, it's only the common birds that really count, isn't it?" Continually hold up the party by calling their attention to robins or hedge-sparrows sitting in huddled attitudes on the vegetation. If after five minutes' observation the robin gives a perfunctory peck at its plumage, say "Nice—an intention movement!" and make notes.

Campbell's third volume will be devoted to Bird Gamesmanship committee meetings, to the use of a pipe [3] at such meetings, and to the art of suddenly

[3] Mention of the use of the pipe in scientific argument and indeed in committee work generally reminds me of the pioneer work on pipemanship of E. Sigsworth of Leeds University (*Yeovil*

saying, without looking at anything or anybody very special, "Do we know that?" quietly but definitely plonkingly. We are grateful to B. Campbell for many of his suggestions here and also for his ready scientific attitudeship when cornered in committee and asked genuine questions about birds. His answer is basically, "I don't know," the Socrates ploy; and these replies

---

Postgraduate Research, Vol. CIV, p. 86): "If you have no advice to give, the pipe will do it for you,"—how often has this been said, but Sigsworth, with his addition of the technique of spittlecraft to the pipeworthy situation, has put order into the chaos of "intuitive" pipe behaviour.

To give an impression of dependable listening it is essential to know *when* to puff smoke, when to go "bup" or "bp" with the lips, and when to take a long noisy wet-sounding blow through an extinguished pipe, to clear the passage.

We usually practise on some young woman who wishes to talk to us in confidence—usually about some love affair. Here is a timed table of pipe effects, with dialogue:

GIRL: . . . and I've often wondered whether I was right to make friends with him even. He would never, I think, think of me in this way. I'm sorry but do I sound to you absurdly silly and pompous over all this?

PIPEMAN: *(puff)*

GIRL: What I should like to do would be to start all over again with him—get back to the mutual interest in work we've always had together . . .

PIPEMAN: *(bup-bup-bup)*

GIRL: What? Do you see what I mean? Because apart from any question of—well, falling in love really with each other—there's always been this—something—between us which is quite outside love—not better or worse but outside of it. I can't talk straight but—do you see . . .

PIPEMAN: *(the long spittle effect)*

If these effects are rightly timed the girl will feel not only that she has been talking well, but that she has never been given such sympathetic advice by such an intelligent listener.

are probably soundly worded and would, I expect, read like this, e.g.:

Q: *Do robins have spotted eggs?*
A: We shall all of us know more about that when we have a longer series to work on.

or

Well, that's really David Lack's specialty, isn't it, and it's a bit sort of—well, awkward—if I go barging in on his territory. Look, I know Lack . . . &c.[4]

or

Ask me in nine months' time. We've got a mass of facts—not yet in very good order.

or

You're taking a terrific lot for granted if you use the word "spot," aren't you?

A Test Case.

B. Campbell draws attention to the gambitous nature of the tendency of that very O.K. Birdsman N. Nicholson to call birds by somewhat archaic though of course perfectly authentic names. The wider O.K.ness is involved in this difficult problem. Is it not fundamentally *correct* scientific attitude ploy to give the faintest possible pat on the head to the brightest jewels in the diadem of English verbal beauty? Anyhow that is the Nicholsonian theory. The process according to Campbell is known as "throstling" or "dunnocking" ("dunnock" for "hedge-sparrow," "throstle" for *Turdus philomelos clarkei clarkei*

[4] P. Scott is also decidedly an O.K. birdsman name. Which of the two is actually the robin specialist is not known.

clarkei). But long ago during an abortive aeroplane trip I gave it the rank of ploy with the name "smale foulesmanship"—and the name has stuck.

I have said enough I hope to show that Birdsmen are natural Lifemen. The kind of question we shall be dealing with in 1953 is Counter-birdsmanship, and it will certainly be one of our headaches. The W.W.W.'s (Windermere Watcher Watchers) are a small Lakeland society who try and force ornithologists into the one-down position by observing them, taking little notes about them, publishing minute pamphlets about them, writing letters to the *Telegraph* about their first appearance, &c. I believe they have had some slight success. For myself I prefer the Return to Nature Poetry approach, and write J. Fisher [5] letters about fledgling voices in the vocal grove. But looking back over the years, I have to admit that this has been only partially successful.

[5] Another O.K. bird name, though one is bound to admit tnat Fisher frequently broadcasts, and in programmes which are liked.

XI

Troutmanship

WHAT A COMPLEX WORLD is here! Yet in the relatively small province of our little Correspondence College, we have made enormous headway and gained the thanks of all the fishership community by defining once and for all the two basic trout approaches, in one of which students are expected to satisfy the examiners.

Our Decontamination Reader in Trout, J. Hargreaves, is a pleasant teacher who plays the two-approach system admirably himself. With newcomers, he demonstrates this twoness with a pair of ordinary fishing rods, one of which is new, the other old.

Rodmanship.

This basic gambit is, basically, the art of being one up with one's rod. Most commonly, the man who still keeps his old rod is pitted against the man who has just bought a new one. Old Rod makes first move:

OLD ROD (*looking at New Rod's new rod*): I like it. I like it. I like it. Of course I'm in my forties. I suppose my old one will see me through. Ought to. Ought to. Ought to.

NEW ROD (*countering implied criticism*): I was sorry to see my last rod go . . . But if one really *fishes* in water like this . . . you know . . . I suppose one kills about a rod a season? Mind you, if you don't go in for these acrobatic casts I'm always attempting, rather unsuccessfully . . .

OLD ROD (*pretending to suspect origin of rod and holding it in his hand*): Tell me—where did you . . . (*Our inflection for "where did you" can imply not only that rod was mass produced, but stamped out of synthetic wood.*)

NEW ROD: Well—you know—"Jackie" Bampton happens to be rather a friend of mine. And my difficulty is that I'm not really comfy unless the action is, well, inches nearer the butt than normal . . .

OLD ROD (*out-gambited but fighting back*): Don't worry . . . don't worry . . . it's like a woman. You get used to it. In a couple of years, anyhow, it will be part of you. Even if you don't catch many trout.

If New Rod's rod is longer, with a longer line, and if the river needs such a rod, Old Rod will be in difficulty. Spandrel's Underthwart can be used here.

SPANDREL (*old rodding*): Nice rod, but it isn't alive till you're about fifteen yards out. I like to throw a shorter line myself.

With right inflection, O.R. can suggest that he is an ancient almost neolithic virtuoso of the trout stream, a sort of Red Indian, really, belly to the ground, who finds no difficulty in trout work at ten yards.*

Troutmanship Basic.

After practice in the two-approach system with rods, students may then start practising troutmanship proper.

This, too, is essentially an A *vs.* B situation. A the purist, the scholar of dry fly, *vs.* B the rough and ready, the ham, the hack.

* Rodmanship Advanced for 1952. This year has seen New Rod placed in the one-down position by Newer Rod Still. This instrument is made of molecularly reconstituted toilet soap. And though it is associated with wrong-clothesmanship (jacket and trousers clean, and matching) and wrong-gadgetmanship (fly-boxes made of perspex), the thing works. We are struggling with this embryonic counter:

NEWER ROD STILL: Yes, it's the first time these fish on the far side of the bend have had a fly decently presented to them.
COUNTERER: Well, I'm bound to admit it makes fishing easier.
N.R.S.: It certainly does.
COUNTERER: I mean, you *could* use a Mills bomb, I suppose.

Tell me frankly, says A the purist, *were you fishing the water or the rise?*

To counter this accusation of just chucking about, the student trained in Old-Rodship should have no difficulty. I'm bound to say that Gattling-Fenn was at his best in this situation. Shirt open to the waist and apparently nut-brown to the navel (actually he wore a "Suntan Gypsyvest"), Gattling was able to imply "For Heaven's sake."

"For Heaven's sake," he said, and the gleam of his almost suspiciously white teeth suggested, "I'm just a hobo, son, a tramp. My father, and his father before him [1] were born natural hunters to a man, like every Englishman born a mother's son."

While suggesting every word of this, Gattling was at the same time able actually to say:

"I had him in a corner—and—yes, I'm bound to say the fly was a bit damp! Spam Special. Yes, I had to rob the sandwich . . ."

The following Hargreaves Hampers are worth study and are useful to others besides troutmen.

1. Do not cast in presence of other fishermen. Proved odds are 93 to 1 against anything happening. So if A says:

A: "Have a go at him."

You, B, should reply either:

B (i): "No—you. I had a good day yesterday."

[1] This would be Gattling-Fenn's grandfather.

or

B (ii): "Oh, that one? He's nearly had me once already. Ruddy great chub."

2. For use against man who catches fish bigger than yours in same water.

TROUTMAN: That's a good one. What does it weigh?
LAYMAN (*cool*): I don't carry scales.
TROUTMAN: I'll weigh it for you . . . one and three quarter pounds. That's funny. How long is it?
LAYMAN: Frankly I don't carry a tape measure either.
TROUTMAN: I do . . . Thought so. Under sixteen inches. That's the trouble with this water, it won't stand fish this size. Ought to be two pounds. It's gone back.

Layman begins to realise he has caught a fish almost on its knees and practically fainting for want of food. He could have picked it out of the water with his bare hands.

3. Rub it in. If for instance rival makes clumsy cast, go on and on pointing it out. Thus:

TROUTMAN (*smiling through clenched teeth*): *Now* you've put him down. Now you *have* put him down. Crikey, were you trying to brain him? Doubt if he'll put his nose up for a week. Should think he'd rather drown. I'll move upstream a bit, I think. Happens to all of us.

Marshall's Mangler.

This subject is still very "young" as we call it at Yeovil—i.e., there is still a lot of loose fishing play within our orbit, and a dozen gambits not yet properly described. That is why I am glad to mention Marshall's "Mangler"—a gambit invented by H. Marshall and needing a finesse and urbanity of execution which totally belies its sobriquet.

The general object is to express an enormous Upper Sixthism so devastating that practically no one else can ever speak about fishing again; and it is done in this way.

The catching of your specific fish is *a Problem,* and must be so approached, without fervour, without even enjoyment.

On one side of your equation is your possible fly, x: on the other, certain variables.

Let α = weather forecast

y = weather

y^1 = flow of stream in relation to mean number of solid factory deposits and old cans

β = probable age of trout

o = probable age of fisherman

π = distance of nearest active motor-bicycle or farm tractor

γ = temperature of fish.

Then, by a simple calculation jotted down in a waterproof tent with unrunnable ink on unsmudgable paper, Marshall would get some such equation as this:

$$x = \frac{\gamma^{16}o\sqrt{\alpha^3 y}\ y^1 - 8}{\beta^2 \pi} = \begin{array}{c} \text{Split's Indefatigable} \\ \textit{or} \\ \text{Aunt Mary's Special} \end{array}$$

Hand this result with your rod to the ghillie and walk quite slowly away, leaving him to catch the actual fish. Marshall has learnt to intensify the effect of all this by turning up on the bank in a bowler hat and a dark pin-stripe and a pair of thin, blindingly well-polished black shoes, in which he delicately picks his way through pool and undergrowth.

XII

The Art of Not Rockclimbing

Rock Play of Odoreida.

"Just-a-Scrambleship," as Rockmanship is sometimes nicknamed, is actually taught in the grounds of our College where, between the croquet lawn and the putting green, is an imitation concrete precipice, four-feet high with a three-foot drop to a spring mattress. Believing that demonstration in the field is essential, students are here taught on the spot how to talk about "holds," "grips," and "nice little problems," and how to come unstuck without actually mentioning it.

This art has a special interest for students of Gamesmanship and Lifemanship—not surprising when it is realised that it is the adopted relaxation of G.

Odoreida. Some of Odoreida's gambits are objected to by the older members of our Council, but if "Odoreida" is the name on every rockman's lips, no less is he referred to as chief authority, by ourselves, in that aspect of this art which may be subtitled: "How to climb rocks without actually going up them."

Our Matterhorn [1] Readers, K. Fitzgerald and B. Hilton-Jones, have described in a definitive conversation the technique of Odoreidaism, and from their comments this analysis is borrowed freely.

Students of Gameslife will be aware that in the

[1] The original name remains, although the Matterhorn is no longer an O.K. mountain.

actual playing of games Odoreida, though often seen on the edge of a cricket field, was a complete rabbit. The weight in his pear-shaped figure, although suggesting the attitude of one accustomed to standing at fairly deep mid-off, was so unusually distributed that genuine climbing looked to be, and was, almost impossible. Besides it is known that on heights he once said he was "frightened he might throw himself over."

It was therefore plucky of Odoreida to life his way into this reputation of his as a skilled rock-climber.

How did he do it?

Odoreida Rock Basic is to be the Man Looking On. Older, now, he is inclined, he tells us amusedly, for slippers. In that little place at Pen-y-gwryd, he is never very far from the fire.

There he will be knowledgeable about past climbs, or present routes. "Yes," he says. Odoreida is encouraging at first. "I do consider the bottom pitch of Charity to be harder than anything on Cloggy." He speculates. "You know [making the wet sucking noise on pipe (see p. 120)] I've always thought the wall on Craig Yr Ysfa would go."

At this point an absolute stranger or complete new boy might begin to call Odoreida "sir."

"Would you, sir?"

"Well, one or two of us saw it the other day on a top rope. I think it would go. By the way, I see you are still using those nails."

New Boy is made to feel the nails in his boots are unsafe, or out of date. Having by this and that prepared a Lifeman's wicket, Odoreida goes in to bat. Essentially this is climb-avoidance play, while seeming to be eager. I know all Yeovil men will want to join with me in emphasising the importance of this gambit.

The H'm Tinge.

Maybe he's not going to climb just now because it's the wrong time of year. In June, Odoreida says, "I only like Great Gully at Christmas time when it's full of ice." At Christmas, on the other hand, he recalls that everyone's done it every Christmas, and that everyone is doing it now. In fact its pretty well got Stop-and-Go lighting.

Somebody else says something else is a difficult climb.

"Well—I seem to remember when Jack did it he did Sunset afterwards. After all the Caldecott brothers took 140 pounds of photographic equipment along that ledge in 1903."

A "h'm" climate is built up.

"The Sceptre presents the same problem—only I suppose ten times more tricky. But I was rather surprised to find ironmongery all over the cilff—the whole place is getting bunged up with it. Bad as the

Matterhorn. Look, I found this half way up Great Slab the other day. Look."

I knew that Odoreida always keeps a rusty piton, scarcely an O.K. climbing aid in this district, always in his pocket, and that he casts doubts on actual climbers by "finding" it. Occasionally he has a rather technical way of saying a boot climb ought to be done in rubbers (or vice versa). Thus:

"No, I don't think so."

So few climbs seem worth while to Mr. Odoreida, thinks New Boy.

"No—I should have to take my rubbers. And it's essentially a boot climb. But the holes are so worn now. But you go, if you want a nice scamper in a pair of gym shoes. I've got my *War and Peace*."

"Good old Wagger-Pagger," replied Gattling-Fenn once, knowing that Odoreida had never read this book, though he was always being found with it, in chimney corners.[2]

If really pressed Odoreida would be quite frank about it. "No," he would say. "Frankly I'm frightened of it."

LAYMAN: Don't blame you. Hardly any holds of any kind, are there?

[2] Odoreida's only genuine reading, besides the *Rockclimbers' Record,* which he memorised for its technical terms, was *Whitaker's Almanack,* where he liked to check up on the salaries of his many acquaintances in the Civil Service.

O: Well, the holds which do arrive, arrive well. Not holds perhaps—certain helpful rugosities . . . But . . . no, I've got my family and I think if one's got a family . . .[3] No. For me Pinnacle Wall is out of bounds.

The danger of Odoreidaism was shown when he sometimes almost convinced *himself* that he was or had been an expert climber, and began talking himself dangerously near to having to make a climb himself. But he could always take refuge in the "frankly I'm getting older" defence.

"The trouble is," he might say, after dinner, "I get so tired standing on one leg looking for the next hole. Coming down I wanted to smoke—but I was finger-jamming all the way . . ."

The New Boy may move in closer, now, to listen. "Only the crook of a finger between Odoreida and eternity," he thinks to himself.

Feeling himself in form, Odoreida might now develop the Other Interest move.

"No. This was in 1936. I thought an off-day was about due . . . and I heard that that lovely little Alpine ranunculus mentioned in Butcher, a kingcup in miniature, had been seen on the Devil's Cliff in 1876

[3] The only person this could possibly refer to is Odoreida's sister-in-law, bolster-thighed Paulette Odoreida, whom he only saw once a year when he took the Odoreida children to the annual opening of the Chelmsford roller-skating rink.

. . . and of course I knew that Hanging Garden Gulley has been stripped to the bone by botanists from the local high school I guess . . . so I thought I'd have a look at the Kitchen proper . . . and there it was, well, just inside the mouth. I think I shall always remember it—seeing that flower."

I heard this and of course was simply waiting for the laugh. Odoreida and spring flowers!

"How did you get *there,* Odoreida?" I said.

Somebody said "Sh!" Odoreida turned smiling towards me.

"Oh, I went up the first couple of pitches of Advocate's Wall, then broke out to the Jut for about thirty feet . . ."

SELF: That's new, surely . . .

O: Well as a matter of fact I think it probably is . . . Having to finish up the wall was too sticky altogether for what I call good climbing.

NEW BOY: But that's one for the log, isn't it?

O: My days for logging climbs are over—that's for you younger people. But I'm afraid it is known, now, isn't it, as Odoreida's Rib? Of course I wanted it called after Messinger because he first saw it. And it was only chance that I found myself on it at all. The whole thing reminds me of the day I nearly got stuck in Lockwood's chimney.

I couldn't help joining, though for different reasons, in the respectful smiles which followed this, and made no use of my private knowledge that years ago Odoreida, lost in the mist when going to post a letter, really did get stuck near the foot of the climb, and insisted on being pulled out by three lady members of the Pinnacle Club and a Brownie.

XIII

Clubmanship

THAT SO TYPICAL institution of this Island, Clubs, has aptly been described as the normal field of exercise, if not the happy hunting ground, of the astute Lifeman. Knowledge of some Club play therefore is considered an essential qualification for Lifemastership.

I propose in this chapter first briefly to outline Club Basic and then to analyse only one, but a very important one, of the main gambits which are essentially Club and which *for that reason* (and because the particular is the only true general) have the wide application always implied in the local.[1]

[1] The local referred to in this paragraph is of course the **Black Lion**.

1. CLUB BASIC

The Two-Club Approach.

Clubmanship proper consists, I always believe, in the continuous implication that you have Another Life, so that even if you dig into your Club regularly at 11:45 A.M. every day and stay there till, dazed with smoke, you feel your way out at midnight, you can still give the impression that it is a question of dropping in for a moment's rest, quiet drink, or chat in between violent spasms of key jobs or valuable social activity.

Certain coarse and obvious ways of trying to show your important independence we have denounced as Sloppy Lifemanship. It is quite wrong to bustle into the Club and tell the Hall Porter that if any messages come through you're "not in." The porter will know and may even say that there have been no messages, not even a letter, for eight weeks. Unsubtle and vulnerable, this approach is termed by us *Lifecorny*.

Never make the mistake, either, of not remembering who your fellow clubmen are. On the contrary know the names and, if possible, the salaries, of everybody, especially if they don't know who you are. Take an interest in their professions. Be actually extremely nice to any crotchety club servant there happens to be and to unusually old members, particularly if they are expiring. It is by such little gracious acts, combined with enquiries about "that nephew of yours with chronic nosebleed" that one-upness is established. Then you can pounce.

Basic Club Play as we teach it is the Two-Club approach. In other words it is essential to belong to two clubs if you belong to one club. It doesn't matter if your second club is a 5/-a year sub. affair in Greek Street; the double membership enables you, when at your main or proper club, to speak often in terms of regretful discrimination about the advantages of your Other One.

But for those who play the genuine Two-Club Forcing Approach, both clubs should be roughly of equal standing, and, if possible, O.K. Then, if the two clubs are of sufficiently contrasted character, which they must be, a fascinating set of ploys can be brought into operation. The essence of the technique of course is to maintain the condition of being, as F. H. Bradley, genial Old Mertonian, once wrote in another context—"the other in the other."

I.e., supposing your two clubs are called, to use a thin disguise, the Artillery and the Studio Arts, basic play is to appear in the artistic club very much a member of the military. Exhibit quite a light touch, in the modern military manner, at the Studio, but maintain a basically clipped appearance, hair short-looking, with bowler hat and the correct clothes for the West End. Ask somebody to "explain" the work of H. Moore, and listen quietly attentive as if knowing perhaps a bit more than you let on, but remain definitely incisive and a well-disciplined club man, silent in the silent room, snookering quietly in the snooker room, drinking soberly at the bar.

When, however, at the Artillery, be quite different, in fact the opposite. Be enervated from your pottery designing at Cheswich, in huge red corduroys and an indigo shirt. Early on, perhaps, you have pointed yourself out by presenting a picture, a particularly abstract abstract, "Paris 1926," to the committee. Already it hangs, if in a very dark corner, near the Lucy Kemp-Welch picture of the Omdurman charge. In mien you are, perhaps, suffering, in accordance with the view which you think Artillery holds of the way the artist behaves. You are certainly abstract. Walking into the Library, a man who has specialised in this work, Hugo Coating, suddenly holds his hand over his eyes and says, "Oh my God." When he said it again at the other end of the library a Lieut.-General Broax said, "What are you 'My Godding' about?"

"I think perhaps . . ." began a more sensitive member—a young captain in the Light Ack Ack.

"I'm sorry but I praised something I thought was bad. Something that I knew really, was bad. Oh God."

"Oh yes," said Broax.

"That is the only untruth."

"How about a cordial?" said Broax, with a look of rough sympathy, seeing that Coating had flung himself face downwards on the settee and kept knocking the arm of it with the instep of his upturned foot. And Coating was often being timidly offered drinks in this way, and though he seldom offered the other half, before long he was able to do what he liked in the Artillery and was a sort of authority, and it was taken for granted that it was perfectly O.K. for Coating to sit in the seat with arms at the head of the long table. Coating became as respected at the Artillery for his arts background as he was at the Studio Arts for his "in the services" tone.

THE TWO-CLUB FORCING APPROACH (1)

Hugo Coating at the Studio Arts dressed as a member of the Artillery.

143

THE TWO-CLUB FORCING APPROACH (2)

The same man (Hugo Coating) at the Artillery dressed as a member of the Studio Arts.

2. A GAMBIT ANALYSED

The Affair at the Monosyllable.

Queer aspects of Clubmanship, extraordinary instances, are often brought to our notice by students and their treatment becomes part of our regular teaching. No harm, now, in revealing that G. Odoreida, with his revolutionary but often coarsely effective Lifemanship of the Left, has a brother, V. Odoreida (husband of rocking-horse-nostrilled Paulette Odoreida) who, it is now well known, is still further to the Left than his brother G. Heaven knows we do not recommend the ploys and gambits of this man for the use of genuine Lifemen, but there is no sense in denying that they exist.

"The Monosyllable" is not the real name of a club. It stands nevertheless for one of the genuinely exclusive Clubs the names of all of which, Lifemen will have observed, are, lifishly enough, only one syllable long.[2] Only Cogg-Willoughby, of our staff, has succeeded in making the membership of one of these. But G. Odoreida of course scoffed and V., his brother, was almost maddened by Cogg's success. He determined on a counter. An incident occurred which we may as well outline. As the members of the Monosyllable were trickling one by one towards the dining room, a message came for Cogg.

"Your guest has arrived, sir."

Cogg stopped in midstream to look around. Had he forgotten? Who? A voice came.

"Hallo, Len, I'm sorry I'm late."

Cogg turned like a shot at this hated abbreviation of a Christian name he had always tried to suppress. A dozen members must have turned with him to see V. Odoreida standing with a long coil of ticker-tape paper held before steel-rimmed spectacles and wearing a shirt slightly soiled and *open at the neck, no tie*.

Cogg had just enough presence of mind left to blurt out, "Thank you. And could you clean the plugs

[2] According to H. Ibsen, translator into Norwegian of W. Archer's translations from the Norwegian, the Founder may be referring to Buck's or White's, Brooks's or the Turf.

as well?" But he felt few were deceived. He rushed from the scene, leaving by some servants' exit. But the damage to Cogg's confidence was lasting. It was at least three months before he next visited the Monosyllable.

XIV

Winesmanship

Definitions.

WINESMANSHIP WAS ONCE listed as a department of Clubmanship. But although it is itself only a province, though a vast one, of the area roughly defined as the Gracious Living Gambit of Lifemanship, Winesmanship may play a big part, sooner or later, in the lives of all of us.

A schoolboy definition of Winesmanship is "How to talk about wine without knowing a hock from a Horse's Neck." But in fact Winesmanship is itself a philosophy if not an ethic, and can be used in Young Manship, in Jobmanship, even in wooing.

Winesmanship Basic.

A few phrases and a ploy or two, to get our bearings. Consider the simplest approach first. If you are taking a girl, or even a former headmaster, out to lunch at a restaurant, it is WRONG to do what everybody else does—namely to hold the wine list just out of sight, look for the second cheapest claret on the list, and say "Number 22, please." Never say the number anyhow, because it suggests that you are unable to pronounce the name of the wine you are ordering. Nominate the wine in English French, and make at the same time some comment which shows at least that you have heard of it before. Say, for instance:

"They vary, of course, but you seldom get a complete dud."

Or simply:

"I wonder . . ."

A useful thing is to look at the wine list before the waiter comes and say "Amazing. Nothing here you can be sure of. Yet the food is quite good. But I've got an idea."

Then, when the waiter comes, say to him "Look. You've got a Chateau-Neon '45 somewhere secreted about the place, I know. Can you let us have a bottle?"

(You know he's got it because you have in fact read it off the wine list, cheapest but one.)

When the waiter leaves you can say, "They keep a little câche for favoured customers."

With a little trouble a really impressive effect, suitable for average city-man guest, can be made by arriving fifteen minutes early, choosing some cheap ordinaire, and getting waiter to warm and decant it. When guest comes say, "I know you'll like this. Should be all right. I got them to get it going at nine o'clock this morning. Not expensive but a perfectly honest wine—and a *good* wine if it's allowed to breathe for three or four hours."

For Home Winesmanship, remember that your mainstay is hypnotic suggestion. Suggest that some rubbishy sherry, nine bob, is your special pride, and has a tremendously individual taste. Insist on getting it yourself "from the cellar." Take about four minutes uncorking it. Say, "I think decanting destroys it," if you have forgotten, or are too bored, to decant it. Keep staring at the bottle before you pour it. When you have drawn the cork, look particularly hard at the cork, and, of course, smell it.

For the first sip of the wine, here are some comments for Student Winesmen. Remember, if the wine is claret, 1920 St. Emilion Chateau Cheval-Blanc, that strangely enough absolutely everybody is supposed to know whether it is a claret or a burgundy. Remember also that practically absolutely everybody is supposed to recognise instantly the year. Practically almost absolutely everybody should be able to say "St. Emilion." The only tiny shade of doubt which can enter your comment is about its being Chateau Cheval-Blanc.

Don't say too much about the wine being "sound" or "pleasant"; people will think you have simply been mugging up a wine-merchant's catalogue. It is a little better to talk in broken sentences and say, "It has . . . don't you think?" Or "It's a little bit corn-ery," or something equally random like "Too many tramlines." I use this last phrase because it passes the test of the *boldly meaningless*.

An essential point to remember is that everybody is supposed to take it for granted that every wine has its *optimum year* up to which it progresses, and beyond which it falls about all over the place. E.g., you can give interest to your bottle of four-and-sixpenny groc-er's port by telling your guest that you "wish he had been able to drink it with you when it was at the top of its form in forty-nine." Alternatively you can say, "I'm beginning to like this. I believe it's just on the brink." Or I rather like saying, "I drink this now for sentimental reasons only . . . just a pleasant residue, an essence of sugar and water—but still with a hint of former glories. Keep it in your mouth for a minute or two . . . see what I mean?" Under this treatment, the definitive flavour of carbolic which has been surprising your guest will seem to him to acquire an interest if not a grace.

Alternatively you may admit, frankly, that your four-and-sixpenny is a failure. "They were right," you say. "The Twenty-fours should have been wonderful. Perfect grapes, perfect weather, and the *vestre*—the Dordogne wind. But for some reason or other they mostly sulked. Taste it and tell me what you think. You may like it."

Or if your four-and-sixpenny is only two years old and unbearably acid you can say, "Let it rest in your mouth. Now swallow. There! Do you get it? That 'squeeze of the lemon,' as it's called . . ."

Then, if there is no hope whatever of persuading Guest that what he is drinking has any merit whatever, you can talk of your bottle as an Academic Interest treat.

"Superb wine, but it has its periods of recession. Like a foot which goes to sleep, has pins and needles, and then recovers. I think that was André's [1] explanation. At the moment it's BANG in the middle of one of its WORST OFF-COLOUR PERIODS."

Watch your friend drink this wine, and if he shudders after it, and makes what we winesmen call "the medicine face," you can say . . . "Yes! You've got it? Let it linger a moment."

"Why?" says Guest.

[1] André Simon, completely O.K. wine name.

"Do you notice the after-sharpness, the point of asperity in the farewell, the hint of malevolence, even, in the *au revoir?*" If he says "Yes," as he will, be pleased.

WINESMANSHIP: A LITTLE-KNOWN PLOY

After saying "I'll get it from the cellar" (not of course really having a cellar), enter any cupboard (preferably beneath stairs), *close door,* and make sound with feet as if descending to (and, after pause, mounting from) a wine cellar.

Note on Tastingship.

Many Yeovil Lifemen are so completely ignorant of wine of all kinds that in our small pamphlet AC/81 we have had to tell them that the red wines are red in colour and, confusing point, the white yellow. It may not be out of place if I remind general readers here, too, that *method of drinking* is an essential accompaniment to *method of comment*.

Before drinking or rather, sipping the wine, you smell it for bouquet. *Not* with a noisy sniff but *silently and delicately,* perhaps making a funnel of your hands to concentrate the essence. G. Gibbs used to create some effect by smelling the stem of the glass as well, but there is no real point in this. A good general rule is to state that the bouquet is better than the taste, and vice versa.

In sipping, do not merely sip. Take a mouthful and chew it, making as much noise as you can. Having thus attracted attention, you can perform some of the evolutions favoured by that grand old Winesman Bath-Meriton. The most ordinary method he used was to lean his head forward so that his rather pro-

THE BATH-MERITON POSITION FOR DRINKING FROM FAR SIDE OF GLASS

tuberant ears were extended like the wings of a monoplane and drink the wine from the far side of his glass. To get the bouquet he would smell it first with the left nostril, closing the other with his forefinger, and then with the right. He would also hold it up to the light and then shine a small pocket torch containing what really looked like a miniature fog lamp through from the other side! He would dip the end of his handkerchief in the wine and then hold the dipped end up to the light. And then, when it actually came to the tasting, he would sip from the *far* side of the glass. Gattling-Fenn once said, "Why not simply turn the glass the other way round?"

Winesmanship Advanced.

The average guest, who knows no more about wine than the Winesman himself, can be easily impressed by such methods. But there are men who genuinely know something of this subject, and they are a very different problem.

I used to advise a simple and direct approach with such people, including an anglicising of the simplest French words (e.g., call the Haut-Brion the High Brion). Gattling-Fenn at his first Saintsbury Club dinner realised that it was 1,000 to 1 the man on his left knew more about wine than he did. So he said (of an old burgundy), using the recommended Ordinary Approach:

"Like it?"

EXPERT: Yes.
GATTLING: It's good.
EXPERT: Yes, but you know what's happened?

GATTLING: Yes—in a way. What?

EXPERT: It's been poured through the same strainer that they used for the Madeira.

Gattling broke into a hearty laugh at this, which quickly froze as he realised from the puzzled faces round him that the expert was speaking seriously.

No—the only method with the true specialist is what we call Humble Studentship, mixed in with perhaps *two* carefully memorised genuine advanced facts.

There are however lesser specialists, semiamateurs, perhaps trying a little amateur winesmanship on their own, for whom we recommend the following advanced methods.

1. *Beaded-bubbleship.* This obscurely titled ploy is merely the art of speaking and especially writing about wine as if it was one of the O.K. Literary Things. Be vague by being literary. Talk of the "imperial decay" of your invalid port. "Its gracious withdrawal from perfection, keeping a hint of former majesty withal, as it hovers between oblivion and the divine *untergang* of infinite recession."

Smiling references to invented female literary characters are allowed here. "The sort of wine Miss Mitford's Emily would have offered Parson Square, sitting in the window-seat behind the chintz curtains."

2. *Percentageship* is, of course, the opposite method,

and designed to throw a different kind of haze, the figure fog, over the wine conversation. Remarks like "The consumption of 'treated' vermouth rose from 47.5 in 1924 to 58.9 in 1926 . . ." will impart a considerable degree of paralysis to any wine conversation. So will long lists of prices, or imaginary percentages of glucosity in contrasted champagnes, or remarks about the progress in the quality of cork trees, or the life-cycle of *Vinoferous demoliens*, little-known parasite now causing panic in the Haut-Baste.

It is always possible, if a wine completely stumps you, to talk in general terms about winemanly subjects.

If it is a warm summer day, remark that "dear old Cunoisier will be getting worried about the fermentation of his musts." [2]

But if in real difficulties, remember that there are moments when the pickaxe is a more useful instrument than the most delicate surgeon's forceps. And I shall always remember Odoreida thrusting aside sixteen founder members of the Wine and Food Society with a "Well, let's have a real drink," and throwing together a mixture which left them breathless. "Pop-

[2] If you have reason to think that your guest is not particularly up in American madeiras, quote the following words in a plonking voice: "There was an 1842 which Sohier took the trouble to bring all the way to London from Boston and gave us in 1938 (April 11th) at the Ritz; the voyage had upset it and it had not had time to recover from the shock."

skull, they called it in Nevada," [3] he said, and poured two parts of vodka into one of sherry and three of rum, adding a slice cut from the disc of a sunflower.

[3] A basic subdivision of Winesmanship is the U.S. hard drink gambit and the question of its counters. The U.S. gambit is to be amused when anybody orders sherry, and to flock round and watch it being drunk, particularly in a club at six o'clock. It is an exaggeration to say that they expect the drinker to bring out knitting or start reading Old Mother Goose, but they are interested.

Nevertheless, the deliberate drinking of sherry will wear many U.S. men down, particularly of course if it is mixed with a rather pi-faced lecture on the American "inability to enjoy wine" and a richly exaggerated account of one's own national habits with drink, making your audience really believe that every typical British family serves a different wine at a different temperature at every course.

A wholly different counter to the U.S. icy hard drink gambit, based on the management of religious men, is to go one better. Serve drinks yourself so cold that they are frozen to the glass and have to be filed out and chewed. Let your martinis be mixed in a much stronger proportion of gin to vermouth than six to one, in fact some counter-U.S. experts pour vermouth into the glass and then pour it out again, lightly mopping the sides with their handkerchief, and then fill the glass with what is of course neat gin. Another ploy is to invent some "little drink" or name of a drink which "everybody is drinking in Nevada" (all Americans admire the suggestion that you have been to Nevada). Call it not "Frozen Larynx" or "Surgeon's Knife," which is 1937–8, but Martini, mixing two absolute disparates as in the Odoreida Iceberg described above. Then peck at it and say, "Oh for a real Martini—a big Martini, one you can pull over your head like a jersey" (wording of U.S. Lifeman 46, spoken to me in April, 1952.

XV

Christmas Giftmanship

A VISITOR TO our College may be agreeably surprised to find a tiny room devoted to Present Giving and Good Cheer. Surprised, I say, because sometimes we are given the reputation of being spoilsports at Yeovil, or told that our Science is a dour one.

Not a bit of it. We have many laughs in and out of hours; and good nature and geniality, at the right season, are encouraged to reign—encouraged, of course, so long as the Lifeman retains his prior right of one-upness.

All of us think of Christmas, particularly, as a time when the spirit of friendliness, of being unusually nice to children especially, should prevail. Yet the alert Lifeman, even at this time of the year, apparently so unfavourable to basic gambiting, knows that he can make the recipient of his niceness feel unpleasant, if slightly.

It was Gattling-Fenn, good Lifeman and great Christmas expert, known for his Favourite Uncle play (see *Lifemanship,* p. 104) who first described the "Remember Mrs. Wilson" gambit (see the special edition of *Lifemanship* printed for the Vassar Foundation). Gattling, by exploding comic sausages, would rouse the children to a pitch of frenzy and then suddenly tell them not to make too much noise because of Mrs. Wilson, a mythical invalid.

It was only last year, however, that I realised the delicacy of Gattling's actual technique with the actual giving of presents.

If I may summarise Gattling-Fenn, the object of Christmas Giftmanship is:

1. To make it seem to everybody present that the receiver is getting something better than he has given you.
2. To make the receiver feel that you have got away with a present that looks all right but which he knows isn't really.
3. To make the receiver feel there is some implied criticism about the present you have chosen.

To take the last section first because it is the simplest and the easiest to explain: a rather dowdy-looking and badly made-up woman who prides herself on "not always dabbling herself with a powder-puff" can in certain tones of voice effectively be given the present of a beauty box. Conversely, a woman who is insidiously ostentatious about the flowerlike and impersonal quality of her beauty can be given a hot water bottle, a small biscuit-coloured Shetland shawl to wear in bed, or a tin of patent food which announces clearly on the front label that it has been specially treated to be made more easily digestible. Add a shopping bag (a group of friends may arrange together to give this lot as a set) and the effect is almost bound to be annoying over a long period and especially in retrospect. Particularly if, thrown in with the rest, somebody can give her one cheap lipstick smelling of lard.

Under this same head come special presents to men who fancy themselves remarkably young for their age. A spectacle case, for instance, for the man unwilling to disclose the fact that he wears glasses; or best of all, a small "YOU AND ME" sound amplifier "which anybody over the age of twenty-five is bound to find useful when listening to conversation in a noisy crowded room." [1]

For the going-one-better ploy, one must act quickly and buy the present for the giver immediately one has received the gift. If a man gives you (if you are a woman) a handbag, you should give him a cigarette case *with initials on it* to hint that you have taken

---

[1] A good deal of work has been done on the dialogue for this particular item. This was demonstrated in the Fourth Lifemanship

more care and he must do better next time. If somebody gives you one of those *de luxe* editions of Jane
Austen in a stand-up cardboard case, you can immediately buy any old nineteenth-century copy of a
George Eliot novel and make the Jane Austen giver
feel he is merely a trier by telling him you have
hunted four years for this example "of the Bristol
edition" (you can call it a "Bristol first"), and that
when you found it six months ago you knew he

Lecture ("Sloppy Yuleship"). Here is the actual dialogue or parlette:

LIFEMAN *(Handing small strangely shaped parcel)*: Happy Christmas.
LAY RECEIVER: What?
L: I said "Happy Christmas." Something for you.
L. R.: Oh, I say . . . *(Paper unwrapping)* What on earth . . .
L: Like it?
L.R.: Yes. What is it?
L: Try it. No . . . look . . . put this little thing in your ear. It's
    a sound amplifier.
L.R.: What for?
L: It amplifies sound. When it's difficult to listen—in a crowded
    room—put it in your ear and wear the battery in your button-
    hole—do you see? Let me . . . it's not a real carnation, it's only
    a dummy—and if you have the least difficulty in hearing . . .
L.R.: But I'm not . . .
L: No, of course you're not. Of course you're not. Of course you're
    not. But—anyone over the age of twenty-five, really, finds it
    difficult to hear in a crowded room. It's not that you're deaf.
    Here. Let me talk to you through it. *(Then recite some poem
    very loudly but with mouth well to side of microphone of
    machine)*
                There was a boy, ye knew him once,
                Ye cliffs and islands of Winander—
L.R.: Of what?
L: WINANDER. Wonderful, isn't it?
L.R.: Thanks very much.

would be the person to appreciate it. At the same time, Jane Austen will half realise he is being fooled and that you have probably only paid half a dollar for it anyhow.

In more advanced work, poor relations may be maddened by giving them useful presents, like scissors or bradawls. Eminent art critics can be given the World's Best Twenty Masterpieces in Oil, done in rather poor colour reproduction, with the dirty pinks merely brown and the browns merely dirty.

A jolly little poker-work doggie which pops in and out of a kennel shaped like a shoe is a splendid present to give to either (a) a zoologist, (b) a collector of Staffordshire glaze, or (c) a breeder of pedigree poodles. To one's wife, of course, one gives the present one wants oneself—a book on astronomy, for instance, or even one on golf, "in the hope that she will really start to play, now."

A keen gardener, who knows something about gardening, can be enormously irritated by being given a poetry anthology on the theme of garden flowers referring to flowers in the vaguest possible terms and quite often describing spring flowers and autumn flowers coming out at the same time, and vice versa. Golfers who pride themselves on the manly professionalism of their equipment can be given golf mittens embroidered with knitted nosegays.

It is rather a good thing to give expensive presents

(a) to people who think they are helping you financially, or better still (b) to those to whom you owe money.

Any man who prides himself on the period accuracy of his room decoration can be given a crinoline lady to fit over a telephone ("Grenfell's Good Turn").

If a hired servant, give your employer something better than he has given you. If you receive an obviously dud present, such as a cheap china sweet tray, when the giver next comes to the house to dine place her present ostentatiously in the middle, with your own sweet trays (silver, and of obviously better design) grouped round it.

If the boss, it is a good thing to give to your employees a calendar consisting of an owl with little numbers under it which have to be moved every day. They will have to be moved every day.

Wonders can be done with a genuinely old painted tray, one handle of which, however, has been broken off so many times that it consists entirely of glue and falls to the ground after half an hour by its own weight. After handle has come off twice, you can say fairly sharply to recipient: "Yes, I'm afraid it was born in an age when mass-production was unknown."

But Gattling is at his Christmanship best when it comes to the treatment of children. His basic gambit is to give them presents a couple of years below their age group. If the child is continuously burying itself in a corner with *Lord Jim,* give it a book about a wild wolf dog which saves a baby from an eagle. If the boy is in the space-travel, space-ship phase, give him any book in which animals talk and hedgehogs wear a watch and chain. Or to any child over seven, just getting really interested in revolvers and sawed-off shotguns, Gattling may, with that genial twinkle, give a book printed on indestructible paper with special "Childprufe" binding about Duckie the Cock and his adventures in Woolie-Woolla Land.

XVI

Hands-Across-the-Seamanship

**NOTE RING ON LITTLE FINGER OF HAND ON LEFT SUP-
PLIED BY OUR DEPARTMENT OF FOREIGN AMITY WITH
A SMALL POINT ON THE INWARD SIDE, FOR SLIGHTLY
PRICKING THE GRASPED HAND**

IT WAS ONCE said of Yeovil, I think not unjustly, that
"the subject of Foreign Relations is neglected here."
Now each candidate is expected to show some pro-
ficiency in what, reduced to its simplest elements, may

be represented as $\varkappa\lambda$ 3.26084 if "$\varkappa$" is the factor of constant international difference [1] and "λ" the vague desire to be pleasant.

It is not our policy continuously to try to be one up on other nations; but it is our aim to rub in the fact that we are not trying to do this, otherwise what is the point of not trying to do this.

First lessons concentrate on the necessity of always using the same phrases, and using them again and again. No harm in the general reader memorising one or two of them now:

We have a lot in common.

After all, we come from the same stock.

We have a lot to learn from each other.

Plasterman's Approach.

The important thing of course is, when speaking to this man from overseas, to get in with one of these sentences first. No one followed this rule more keenly than Gattling-Fenn's half-brother, who was not called Gattling-Fenn at all but Joe Plasterman—whence the whole gambit-sequence involving the use of those phrases sometimes called "Plasterman's Approach."

It is known that once when Plasterman was a guest at the Monosyllable, he saw two members standing at the bar. He was unknown to these members, *and they were at this time unknown to each other.* But Plas-

---

[1] I.e., the tendency to be faintly superior about foreigners.

terman's host had happened to mention that one of them was an American.

Plasterman went up to these two men and placed his hands gently on their upper arms, standing between them. Quietly he said:

"The future happiness of the world is based on the friendship of the two peoples."

Then, with a slight downward pressure of his hands on the shoulders of the two, he added: "I won't say any more."

"Do you know those two?" said his host, when Plasterman got back.

"Why not? They are my brothers, aren't they?" said Plasterman, still in the Approach position, but he noticed that his host looked as if he was trying to disappear into himself. Host began to whisper:

"But I mean that was Ed Morrow and Harold Nicholson. They can't both be your brothers. Besides . . ."

"However unworthy the sower of the seed . . ." began Plasterman; but his host was beginning to edge off, and Plasterman—fate of the Lifeman—was left alone with his one-upness.

Plasterman's work was quickly recognised and it was not long before he was given a position of trust in the Goodwill Department of the Ministry. It was through Plasterman, actually, that a specifically U.S.

Problem came my way, no doubt because I know the States well myself, having lived there for close on thirty days. It was therefore as Founder of the American branch of Games-Life (Principal, J. Bryan III, of Wa:), in conjunction with the Office of American Enthusiasm, that it became my pleasant duty to greet American visitors to Britain in the Festival Year, and appear to be trying to make them feel at home while at the same time becoming one up on them (G.B.-manship). My pamphlet on the subject has long been delivered to the department concerned and may be printed early in 1965.[2] Here meanwhile is the work of our collateral branch on U.S.manship.

U.S.MANSHIP

A note on how, when visiting Britain, to appear to be quite happy to be one down, while actually remaining one up

General Rules.

The basic gambit for all Lifemen, of course, is to praise. And the basic, because slightly annoying, thing for U.S.men to praise in Britain is its charm. This is sometimes called "Cliffs of Dovership." It can be done with most effect if you praise, and with politeness, the charm or quaintness of any of the following:

[2] My summary will be published in '53, Series IV, *Games-Life*.

(a) Pseudo-Tudor, such as the thatched telephone kiosk on the London-Oxford road, or some frightful old barn which has been casting a shadow over your host's garden for years, shortening the lawn-tennis court by two feet, yet incapable of being pulled down, removed, or destroyed for lack of money, labour, and the necessary pulling-down local government licence.

(b) Some bits of condemned and muddy farm land with neglected coppice and untended rivulet, which local residents are particularly ashamed of.

(c) Something which the British don't think charming at all but on the contrary particularly up-to-date and mechanised and modern. Stand for instance in front of the new London University building, one of the highest in London, and "love it because it's quaint." Watch one of our most renowned and actually streamlined engines, the Bournemouth Queen or the Coronation Scot, steaming out of its terminus, and say, "I've always wanted to see a steam-engine again. Why, I remember when the Twentieth Century Limited used steam." Or ask to be taken on a tour of the largest British film studios, at Denham, and say "Why, it's got everything, cameras, lights, and here's a little—we call it carpenter's shop—too!"

Another good general ploy when in Britain is to take for granted absolute ignorance of anything American, and then be surprised, if not offended, if your British listener has not heard of some name of purely local interest. E.g., say, "We have a magazine called the *New Yorker*," or "There are two President Roosevelts, you know." *Then* talk without any explanation but with a wealth of local details about "Lausche in the days when he was Mayor of Cleveland," and take it for granted that your British friend will not only be interested but informed.

There is a decidedly irritating way of "being amused," very difficult to acquire, yet practised by many a successful U.S.man. He will suggest to his British friend that "like all Britons" he thinks of American history as beginning with George Washington and the cherry tree, leaping straight to the Boston Tea Party, jumping thence to Uncle Tom's Cabin via American Indians being shot down one by one as they circle round Gary Cooper and a band of early settlers who succeeded in preserving America for Sam Goldwyn. This friendly teasing is irritating because it includes and subtends a basic gambit, "Grain of truthship."

Behaviour.

In dress, be either (a) keenly American or (b) extremely English. But note to Bostonians: extreme Englishness is set off rather than spoilt if one Americanism creeps in: e.g., in day dress it is O.K. not to show cuffs: or (recommended American pronunciation inserted in perfected Bostonian English) retain the American *"must*-tash" instead of the relatively feeble English "mstarsh."

It is slightly annoying to the English to be told that their English accent is "perfect" or "sweet" or "cute," since the Englishman rightly believes that he alone has no accent whatever. It is also annoying to the Englishman who prides himself on his clever imitation of the American accent to point out that in fact the accent he is trying to reproduce is a mixture of the dialects of six American States, all of which are not less than fifteen degrees south of the Maine accent to which, from its wording and references, the mimicry seems intended.

BBCmanship.

A habit for which the English will be too polite to reprove the U.S.man is that of bringing his own producer, effects department, and gramophone girl when broadcasting at the BBC.

It has definitely been proved to annoy if U.S.man says to Englishman, "I'm glad to see you've taken on television here—why, of course, you were right in on the start, weren't you?"

Remember (BBCmanship) that all the British can, will, and must pitch into their BBC all the time, but that, conversely, no visitor to England may be allowed to criticise the BBC in the smallest detail. U.S.men desirous to create an awkward pause are safe, then, in slipping into some quite irrelevant conversation some such remark as this:

"You know, you ought to have sponsored radio over here. More snap. More pop. More crackle."

Interest in Cricket.

U.S. visitors must, of course, go to Lord's-sacred-shrine-of-cricket in an attitude of gentlemanly respect and alert anticipation. If they find while watching the game that for the first twenty minutes absolutely nothing happens, they should not comment on the fact that absolutely nothing happens, but they should suddenly turn to their host and say, "You know, we have heard so much about Lord's in the States. Now I want you to analyse for me the wonderful atmosphere which they say pervades this place." After forty minutes, if a batsman scores one run, it is coarse U.S.manship to say "Would Di Mag have powdered that one!" Just say "Wow."

Make some reference, suggesting that an effort is being made, to W. G. Grace, England's greatest genius of cricket, but get one initial wrong, perhaps the second.

Individual Ploys.

When going to a British Railway station do not *say* anything about the relative miseries of these spots, but bring galoshes, blankets, air cushion, packet of sandwiches, and own coffee in a thermos. It is quite a good ploy in England to be seen constantly carrying about coffee in a thermos.

Conversely yet perhaps connected with this, it is rather a good thing, having arrived in Britain by air, to ignore Westminster Abbey, Parliament Square, and the Tower of London when your host mumbles something about these places with vague pride, and say instead, "I can't wait to get to see Waterloo Station."

Carry with you any example of a recent British article criticising America, broadmindedly and genially agree with it, and praise the British for having given such a good example to the Americans of what the Americans ought to have done. E.g., take a recent British *Architectural Review* attack on domestic architecture in the United States and read it out loud to your British friend while standing amidst the housing accretions of any suburb of any large British town or in any recently built village, and say, "Yes, you certainly have got a way with your domestic architecture which we can't touch over there."

It is quite a good thing to read up bits of local history and literary association, then ask your British friend and guide questions about it. Henry VII's Chapel in Westminster Abbey makes a good background for such knowledgable questions. Or Dove Cottage, home of Wordsworth in the Lakes, with special reference to Coleridge's visits there. In both cases, of course, your British host will be unable to conceal his almost complete ignorance of the facts involved.

If your British friends fail to be put off or made to feel slightly awkward by these delicate little gambits, and mutual friendliness and goodwill insist on breaking through, it is always possible to fall back on Anglo-American relations. We at Yeovil are at present formalising this splendid instrument of general dis-ease, gambits, counter-gambits, and the one-up-one-down atmosphere. We are rather proud of our name for it—"Manglo Relations"—which has been formed syncretically from the two terms "Anglo-American Relations" and "mangled feelings." The natural friendliness, the recognition of a home from Home, the geniality and mutual admiration which exists between the two nations, can always be frustrated by anyone who uses the word Relations, with its disagreeable double meaning. This can be brought in indirectly, or insidiously, by expressions based on the phrases students should have memorized from the beginning of this chapter: "The British are our best friends" or "The freedom of the world depends on America and England keeping in close touch, pooling common knowledge and working eye to eye." Whatever phrase you use, the Manglo-Relations Department can always be guaranteed to put temporarily out of joint the firmest and most lasting friendship in the world, and frustrate the un-Lifemanly habit, frowned on at Yeovil and much in evidence recently between British and Americans, of just plain ordinary liking each other.